REINHOLD MESSNER

THE NAKED MOUNTAIN

Nowadays we talk of Nanga Parbat, Batura or K2,
but in the early days of the Han Dynasty these were
known as 'the mountain of bad headaches', 'of terrible
fever', 'of stiff and sore limbs' and 'derangement'.
Chinese researchers look for the reasons for this
strange nomenclature in ancient demonology.

Hermann Schäfer

REINHOLD MESSNER

THE NAKED

MOUNTAIN

TRANSLATED BY TIM CARRUTHERS

THE MOUNTAINEERS BOOKS

Published in North America by

The Mountaineers Books
1001 SW Klickitat Way, Suite 201
Seattle, WA 98134
www.mountaineersbooks.org

Published in the UK by
The Crowood Press Ltd.
Ramsbury, Marlborough
Wiltshire, SN8 2HR

English translation © The Crowood Press Ltd.
First English language edition: 2003

German title: *Die Nackte Berg: Nanga Parbat – Bruder, Tod und Einsamkeit*
© 2002 Piper Verlag GmbH, München, Germany

A cataloging-in-publication record for this book is available at the Library of Congress

ISBN: 0-89886-959-5 (North America)

Printed and bound in China through Bookbuilders.

To Günther, my climbing partner
and my brother.

Günther Messner, 1970

Convoy of climbers and porters on a Himalayan approach march.

Contents

Avalanche on the Diamir Face of Nanga Parbat.

*Nanga Parbat from the west
with the Diamir Face and the
upper Diamir Valley.*

Nanga from the east with Hermann Buhl's 1953 route; to the left is the Rupal Face.

In 1856, Adolf Schlagintweit stood at the foot of the southern precipice of this mountain. In terms of size and steepness there is perhaps no other mountain face on Earth that can compare. I dare to make this statement since Marcel Kurz, one of those best acquainted with the high mountains of the world, shares this view. From the valley floor at Tarshing to the summit it is 5200m of vertical height. As established by Finsterwalder during observations conducted on the 1934 expedition, the average angle of the South-East Face is 47.5 degrees, and on the upper section 68 degrees. Steep indeed!

Paul Bauer

This dark mountain realm with all its hidden threats lies at the end of the source of all that is living.

A.F. Mummery

The Film in My Head

The defining experience of my life happened a long time ago in a faraway place. It was in the Himalaya, on Nanga Parbat, that I experienced the kind of expanded state of being that occurs on two levels of consciousness, the kind that can easily lead you to believe that the brain is suffering from insane delusions. For it was there that I experienced, quite clearly, how Life and Death first occurred and how they then – almost simultaneously – became part of my biography. What happened all those years ago remains in my memory as the story of my own death and at one and the same time the impossible story of my survival.

The traverse of Nanga Parbat from south to north-west in 1970 was, for me, far more than the crossing of a definite line in the geographical sense. It was like a border crossing from this world to the next, from life to death, from death to life.

I am recounting the whole story in detail now, in order to include all those who are a part of what happened and the pre-history that, at a subconscious level, was a part of my experience from the very start.

Back then, I was completely alone for a week – inconsolable, despairing, without hope – as I made my way down into the Diamir Valley. I had suffered, I was badly frostbitten. I had died. Half starved, my soul laid bare, I finally returned to the company of human kind. When I finally saw all the others again, the people I had expected to rescue me, Nanga Parbat seemed far away, an untouched peak above the clouds – the

11

The Mazeno Ridge and Nanga Parbat from the south. The Messner brothers' route is on the right of picture.

Naked Mountain. My brother, too, was far away. But where exactly was I? As I looked around the Indus Valley, I felt longing, fear and pain. I was still here.

When I look back at these events today I see myself both as the victim and the dispassionate observer of the tragedy that befell us. As if I have passed through several stages of consciousness, my survival on Nanga Parbat lives on within me, an intimate interplay between being there and a far-off detachment from the events. I now wish to tell the story of that Nanga Parbat expedition in the same way that I experienced it, as an interplay between pure observation and a story as I experienced it, a shocking tragedy that marked the beginning of my identity as a man who tried to push the boundaries.

The 4000m Diamir Face of Nanga Parbat.

Up there in the summit region, driven only by the will to survive, I frequently saw myself from a distance, as if my spirit had become detached from my body. Then I experienced again how reason and intellect would process emotions and incorporate them into my being, finally to create a feeling of unshakeable certainty. Thus it was that feelings of helplessness and despair became my destiny and a part of my life story.

I do not question what it is that creates this ability to experience events in this way; I am more concerned with the self that was born out of this process. I am telling a story that goes far beyond my own life and I write it down here as I experienced it then, as observer and protagonist at one and the same time. My theme explores how external sensual stimuli and the worry of survival create fear and how a person reacts when caught between the twin forces of life and death.

13

Without consciously wishing to interpret how things occurred in the way they did, I write of the way I experienced my survival and the split between being part of those events and standing apart from them. My brain registered everything that happened in exact detail – the external and the emotional, the physical and the mental processes – as if there were intervals or spaces between the feeling, the realization and the storing of the information.

Although in the final instance these mental leaps were concentrated purely on the human organism's instinct to preserve life – slowed down, perhaps, by the imminent possibility of dying and the lack of oxygen – their effect on my conscious mind was similar to a state of schizophrenia, as perceptions and emotions faced each other like images of the sun and the moon.

In exactly the same way that feelings arise from external sensual stimuli and the experience later remains as a 'film in the head', my story shifts from the first to the third person during the critical phase. Splicing the emotions of the spectator into my 'film in the head' is my attempt to clarify how the conscious self arises when death is close.

Nanga Parbat

Nanga in the early morning light, viewed from the east.

The Nanga Parbat massif forces the Indus to change course and head off at 90 degrees to the south on its 2000km journey from Mount Kailas to the Indian Ocean.

Hermann Schäfer

It was around the middle of the 19th century that Nanga Parbat, the 8125m high western cornerstone of the Himalaya, was first 'discovered' by Europeans. Adolf Schlagintweit, the Munich-born Asian explorer and researcher, had penetrated as far as the foothills of the Himalaya on his travels and had seen Nanga Parbat from the south. A little while later he was murdered in Kashgar. The fateful history of Nanga Parbat had begun...

Reinhold Messner

The South Face of Nanga Parbat, viewed from the Dusai Plateau.

The Most Difficult Climb of My Life

When Adolf Schlagintweit asked the locals about the name of the great mountain he had seen they replied 'Diámar' and 'Nánga Parbat'. Translated from the Urdu, the names mean 'King of the Mountains' and 'the Naked Mountain'.

When, seventy-eight years later, in 1934, the geographer and mountaineer Richard Finsterwalder was able to study the mountain from all sides and carry out an exact survey, he simply referred to it as 'Nanga', in common with most climbers of the time. Finsterwalder, then a professor in Munich, was impressed: 'There is a 7000m height difference between the ice-encrusted peak of Nanga and the Indus, whose melancholy waters wind their turbulent way along the foot of the mountain. There are probably few places on this Earth where nature displays herself to mankind in such a grandiose and varied manner and reveals so much to us of her secrets and wonders.' He went on: 'Nanga Parbat is constructed like a series of storeys, with deeply riven valleys and gloomy gorges scored deep into its mighty body.'

In a similar way to Alexander von Humboldt's description of Chimborazo, the work of Schlagintweit, Finsterwalder and, later, Dyhrenfurth has shaped the popular image of Nanga Parbat. With information gained from their botanical, geological and mountaineering explorations they awakened a similar degree of curiosity about the mountain.

Günther Oskar Dyhrenfurth believed that the Nanga Parbat group was a single, homogenous massif of gneiss and, like Finsterwalder before him, he gave considerable thought to the potential routes of ascent. Dyhrenfurth was effusive about the view he had of the mountain and excited by the

17

Down in the Diamir Valley. Mummery passed this way in 1895. In 1970 Reinhold Messner lay here injured, unable to walk.

BELOW: *The Mazeno Ridge and Nanga Parbat (left), scene of the 1895 and 1970 tragedies.*

idea of the peak as a mountaineering objective. 'The summit is covered in glistening firn snow, the ridges and faces plastered in ice. Beneath these is a belt of alpine pastures and mighty forests that drop down to the glaciers below. Lower down the forests stop suddenly and the vegetation grows sparser. It is hot and dry here and we find isolated little settlements with artificial irrigation. Lower still the heat has killed off all life and right at the bottom of the mountain, the last 1500m down to the Indus, is a fearful desert region.'

18

For explorers and mountaineers alike, the mountain appeared to be an objective full of secrets and mystery. For half a century it represented the greatest possible challenge for the elite amongst German-speaking mountaineers – it became their Holy Grail.

'When German climbers set off to remotest Asia to conquer this peak they would not be true German climbers if merely standing on the summit were enough for them', Finsterwalder suggests. 'If they failed to bring home with them anything of the wonder and mystery of the Himalayas then all the trials and tribulations encountered on the way to this Holy Grail of mountaineering would be for nothing.'

1934. Himalaya. Nanga Parbat. For the first time, five climbers and eleven Sherpas pushed the route as far as the Silver Plateau. Following the route reconnoitred in 1932 they almost got as far as the summit. The leader of this dangerous enterprise was one Willy Merkl; the mood one of expectation and concern. A short while before, Alfred Drexel had died of altitude-induced pulmonary oedema. The team was feeling the pressure. Suddenly the mist closed in and the wind blew up. The snow storm lasted two weeks. The descent was catastrophic: Uli Wieland, Willo Welzenbach, the expedition leader Merkl and six Sherpas lost their lives.

When Karl Maria Herrligkoffer, a younger half brother of Merkl, learned of the tragedy he vowed to continue 'the battle for Nanga Parbat' as a legacy and memorial to his late brother. Willy Merkl was his role model and the heroic death of the Germans on Nanga Parbat provided the impetus for him as he strove to realize the ideals that they had aspired to. For Herrligkoffer, this far-off peak in the Himalayas soon became an obsession.

The locals have two names for their mountain: Nanga Parbat, 'the Naked Mountain' and Diamir, 'King of the Mountains'. Herrligkoffer viewed the mountain as his own personal holy crusade. This unclimbed peak became the

The Rakhiot Face of Nanga Parbat with the Silver Saddle and the Silver Plateau. The summit is on the far right.

objective to which he would dedicate his whole life. This was Nanga Parbat, the mountain of destiny.

Herrligkoffer published the diaries of Willy Merkl and came to identify more and more closely with the lifetime ambition of his brother. In order to redeem his silent pledge he wished to travel to the Naked Mountain himself. Working like a man possessed, he found the financial means and the first-rate mountaineers he needed, acquired the necessary mountaineering permit and organized all the travel arrangements and equipment. In 1953 he undertook his first journey to the Himalaya, leading a group of climbers to Nanga Parbat, the Holy Grail of German mountaineering. The venture was known as the Willy Merkl Memorial Expedition.

Hermann Buhl finally succeeded in making the first ascent of the mountain, against the express wishes of Herrligkoffer. Pepped up by the drug Pervitin he managed 1300m of ascent in a single day, reaching the summit alone on the evening of

View from the Silver Plateau back to the Silver Saddle with the Karakorum in the distance.

3 July 1953. After surviving a night out in the open, he managed to descend safely. With his last ounces of strength he reached the camp below the Silver Saddle, where the two colleagues who had supported him on his summit bid were waiting. Herrligkoffer, however, who as leader of the expedition had previously ordered retreat from the mountain from his position at Base Camp, was in an emotional quandary. His feelings wavered between joy at the success and disappointment in the manner in which it was achieved. He felt he had been betrayed by the three men, who had acted against his instructions, outshone by Buhl, who had acted selfishly on his own account, and passed over by the world media. Perhaps he also felt cheated of the 'unconditional' ascent that the voice of his dead brother demanded of him?

Back in Europe, doubts arose as to the validity of Buhl's summit bid. Herligkoffer even initiated legal proceedings against the 'victorious summiteer' at a later date. In

21

A group of porters on the Abruzzi Glacier in the Karakorum. Broad Peak, Buhl's second 8000m peak, is on the left of the picture.

LEFT: *The summit ridge of Chogolisa in the Karakorum, Buhl's last objective.*

Herligkoffer's eyes, Buhl remained until his death the 'defiler of the pure ideal'.

For Herligkoffer it was the myth of Nanga Parbat that exerted such a magical power and allure. He felt that to capture the prize that rightly belonged to his brother, yet had proved impossible for him to achieve, was his destiny. More and more climbers made the pilgrimage to the 'King of the Mountains' with this obsessive man. It was not that the mountain needed them, they needed the mountain: for their ambitions, their dreams, their hubris. Karl Maria Herrligkoffer had stylized the 'Naked Mountain', elevating it to a high ideal.

It was in this climate of madness that, in 1970, a team set off to attempt the South Face of Nanga Parbat; the highest mountain face on Earth; the holy grail, too, for a young generation

23

PREVIOUS PAGES: *The Rupal Face and photos of the journey: Alice von Hobe, Karl Herrligkoffer, Reinhold Messner, Max von Kienlin; expedition truck in Persia; porters in Tarsching; Base Camp.*

ABOVE: *Felix Kuen and Reinhold Messner leaving Camp 1 on the Rupal Face.*

BELOW LEFT: *Max von Kienlin and Hermann Kühn play chess as Reinhold Messner looks on.*

BELOW RIGHT: *Camp fire at Base Camp; Karl Herrligkoffer on the right.*

OPPOSITE: *A column of porters descends from Camp 2 in new snow.*

ABOVE: *The upper part of the Rupal Face. Beneath the summit to the left is the Merkl Couloir with the Merkl Icefield (Camp 4) below.*

OPPOSITE, TOP TO BOTTOM: *View from Camp 4 down into the Rupal Valley; Günther Messner clearing snow at the Ice Dome (Camp 3); Camp 2 on the Rupal Face.*

OVERLEAF: *At the foot of the dangerous concave sweep of the Diamir Face, Reinhold Messner spent days' searching for his brother Günther before heading down the valley.*

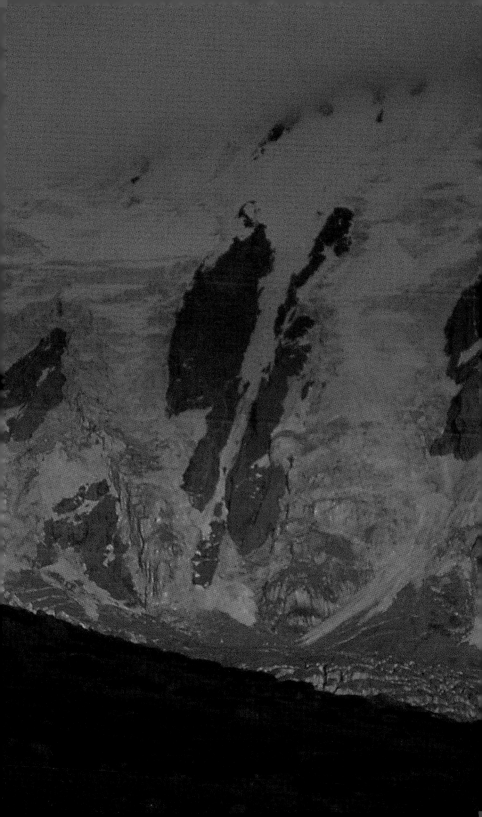

Reinhold Messner searched for his brother in the glacial corrie at the foot of the Diamir Face (top left) before crawling down the dead Diamir Glacier (top right) to the upper Diamir Valley (bottom) and the first flowers and people.

OPPOSITE PAGE: *The summit headwall of Nanga Parbat, viewed from the south.*

32

of mountaineers, for whom Herligkoffer was their only chance of making a successful ascent.

Tensions again arose between the expedition leadership and the summit team and again it came down to a solo summit bid, this time by Reinhold Messner. Messner's brother Günther followed him of his own free will and on 27 June 1970 they reached the summit together. However, Günther succumbed to altitude sickness, and the two brothers were forced to descend by the Diamir Face, at the foot of which Günther perished.

Thus it was that that one man, many miles away from shelter of any kind, alone and abandoned, dragged his exhausted body down the Diamir Valley. Suffering schizophrenic delusions brought on by days without food or sleep, he talked to himself, the trees and the rocks, walking off his loneliness, his fear and desperation. Slipping gradually into the role of dispassionate spectator, he finally observed his own death. In a state of temporary insanity born of loss and desperation he miraculously returned to civilisation, a changed man.

Karl Maria Herrligkoffer, however, still obsessed with Merkl's legacy, viewed Reinhold Messner's descent in the same way as Buhl's ascent all those years ago: as an act of treachery.

Chapter I

My Brother, His Death and My Madness

The South Face of Nanga Parbat, known as the Rupal Face.

Could there be any other mountain face on Earth that is higher than the one captured in the sketches penned by Schlagintweit? The mountain is indeed 'naked', for the fall line of the great flank is almost vertical, so that snow can barely cling to the precipitous slopes.

Hermann Schäfer

The first view is always of the fearsome South Face. 5000m high, with mighty granite buttresses and overhanging domes of ice, it rises up out of the midday mists in the Rupal Valley to the crowning glory, the summit.

Fritz Bechtold

Where the mountains of the Alps and the Caucasus stop, here in the Himalaya is where they start.

Hermann Schäfer

Günther Messner, 1970.

Günther – Lost but not Forgotten

In 1970, the Rupal Face of Nanga Parbat was exactly to our taste – big, steep and a long way away.

When a journalist asked my younger brother about our objective, he received no answer at first. Günther merely looked at him. It was as if he was incapable of imagining the huge mountain face. It was eerily quiet in the room. Günther's silence was a part of his answer. Then he produced a photograph. 'It is very big,' he said.

After the long, pregnant pause and the silence, this one short sentence had an explosive effect. It was almost tangible; the mountain in the photograph seemed to grow infinitely large, like a mountain viewed through a magnifying glass. The journalist asked us what we intended to do out there. Again there was silence from Günther; a long silence. My brother fixed the stranger with his gaze. As he turned to go, after a further, even longer, silence, he uttered a few trivial words: 'Just want to get away from here, far away.'

Günther, my younger brother, is now dead, yet still he lives on in my dreams.

Günther and I are climbing the North Face of the Kleine Fermeda in the Dolomites, in the Geisler group. We have just finished traversing across a snowfield and I am leading off up the vertical summit wall. I have tied the hemp rope directly round my waist and Günther pays it out over his shoulder as he belays me in the classic style.

The North Face of the Kleine Fermeda is the first big face we have climbed independently; we are extremely proud of our independence.

Kleine Geislerspitze from the north. On the right is the Kleine Fermeda.

I move across to the right on loose rock and gain a crack, which ends abruptly at the summit ridge. Beneath my feet the face falls away steeply for hundreds of metres. With my big, clumsy boots I dislodge a small protruding rock, which breaks away and drops with a sharp crack into the void. 'Ten metres of rope left,' Günther shouts.

The sun shines brightly above the shadowy precipice. Leaning forward to peer into the void we can feel the cold thrill of danger. With a few swift, catlike moves I haul myself upwards to stand on the ridge in the sun. Quickly belaying the rope to a knob of rock, I lean out over the face. 'Safe!' I shout.

It is time for Günther to second the pitch.

As I attempted to describe the last route we climbed together the impressions were still so fresh and the loss of my brother so painful that I had alternately to consciously think myself into the role of protagonist and observer in order to prevent myself from succumbing to madness once more. This schizophrenia was like a medicine. And yet, I did not wish to delve again into self pity as I counted off the time backwards to the death of Günther, where everything ended and everything begins.

Then, as now, I feel time stand still whenever Günther is with me. We talk to each other; everything still lies before us. It is as if I have forgotten the intervening years.

During the descent from the mountain after Günther's disappearance I was so immeasurably alone that I constantly held conversations with myself. These were days full of despair and I was talking for my life. It was as if talking alone were enough to give me that faint ray of hope. Talking had become a matter of survival. It was all about getting through just one day, staying alive for just one more day. It was not a question of having died, for in death there is no longer any thought of self. But even as a survivor I still experienced that feeling of increasing remoteness as a feeling of having been abandoned; as a kind of dissociation. Perhaps

this was because one can neither cope with, nor indeed survive, such loneliness without suffering lasting damage.
Günther was dead. I had to get home alone.

In the intervening years, I have retold the whole story a hundred times. Calling to mind the details over and over again, I have tried to hold onto Günther and at the same time let go of him piece by piece. But to have to reduce his death too often to just a few sentences causes me pain. To comprehend the incomprehensible requires time. Now, thirty years later, the contexts become clearer and the backgrounds brighter and more coherent. With the help of diary entries, quotes from official expedition reports (*see* Bibliography, page 315) and letters, I will now tell the story of my mountain of destiny. And so, in a fragmentary way, like the tiny stones of a mosaic, the story of our complete traverse of Nanga Parbat is assembled until a picture emerges that is timeless.

Now that I am prepared to understand my own self as the sum of that which is both within and without, the aggregate of body and soul, I can finally write about the most difficult days of my life – the story of the Naked Mountain.

Chapter II

The Crowning Glory: the Himalaya

The snow ridge leading to the Silver Saddle.

'The crowning glory and the ultimate aspiration of the mountaineer's wistful yearning!' That was how Willy Merkl described the high peaks of the Himalaya. His whole life had been geared towards achieving this objective, yet shortly before he could taste victory an unimaginable destiny had snatched that crown from his grasp.

Karl Maria Herrligkoffer

Willo Welzenbach.

Willy Merkl seized upon the ideas outlined by his friend Welzenbach, whose plan to mount a Nanga Parbat Expedition in 1930 had been frustrated.

Johann Ammer

Now we see it for the first time: Nanga, the mountain of our dreams! The view of the South Face is breathtaking; with a height of 5000m, it must surely be the most enormous of the world's big faces. We have to crane our necks just to get a look at the snow-clad summit, perched high above the awesome precipice of that Face. One thing we know for sure: this is the biggest thing we have ever seen in our lives. Or, rather: never before have we felt so small and insignificant as now, in the presence of a mountain of such unique and tremendous size.

Willy Merkl

The First Attempt

It has a certain fairy-tale sound to it, to be sure. For once upon a time, at the end of the nineteenth century, there was a man who reached for the stars: A.F. Mummery, one of the most prolific English mountaineers of his time. Thus is was that, forty years before the Germans arrived, the first serious attempt was made to bag the first ascent of the Naked Mountain. Incredibly, it was way back in 1895 that Mummery, accompanied by his fellow countrymen Collie and Hastings, and two soldiers from the Gurkha regiment, penetrated the upper Diamir Valley by way of the Rupal Valley and pitched his tents on the edge of the glacier. Directly opposite, on the broad flank of the mountain, he could make out a line of ascending rock spurs, which appeared to form a natural, and certainly highly possible, route of ascent, he thought. Together with the Gurkha Ragobir as his porter and a local hunter, Mummery actually managed to work his way up to a point just above the middle rock spur – in nailed boots, with no pitons either for protection or to safeguard abseil descents. A tent was firmly anchored on the second rock spur and stocked with provisions. After carrying loads to the camp, bad weather brought storms and forced a retreat. A second attempt was mounted and a second food dump made at 6100m. As Mummery and Ragobir were scrambling up onto the crest of the ridge-like upper spur, a large block became dislodged from the balustrades of ice perched above them. At first, there was silence…

Mummery and Ragobir were climbing the steep undercut rib when they were alarmed to hear a deafening crash. Instinctively, they ducked and then rose to their feet again

The Diamir Glacier, looking towards the Diamir Gap.

immediately. High above them, a monstrous mass of ice and snow had gathered and was now bearing down on them, growing in size like a gathering cloud. Seconds later they were enveloped in a boiling white mass of spindrift. From below, through his binoculars, Collie saw only how the two men disappeared under the cloud. He believed them to be dead.

Mummery, too, was fearful that the spindrift avalanche would sweep them off the mountain with it. He whirled around frantically, but could see nothing. There was a crack and a roar, accompanied by flashes of light that lit up the sky for a brief instant. Mummery could only cling on and hope that they would remain unharmed by this thunderous maelstrom of ice and snow.

Ragobir was totally distraught. He could not understand what was happening and was visibly shaken, his whole body trembling violently. 'Pull yourself together, man,' Mummery

View of the Rakhiot Valley from the Diamir Gap.

screamed at his porter, 'It's all or nothing now.' He repeated the phrase under his breath, over and over again, reciting it like a mantra.

Collie watched the plummeting tangle of cloud for a long time. Then he looked up. As the bank of spindrift began to disperse, two figures appeared, moving. They were alive! They were climbing on. Acting like a dam wall, the rock spur had diverted the mass of falling ice to one side and funnelled it down a gully, sparing the climbers above on the crest of the rib.

Mummery, only briefly distracted by the occurrence, felt safe on the rib and climbed on undeterred with the Gurkha. They did not reach the icefield above, however, for a long way below the last difficult band of ice cliffs Ragobir fell ill. The gateway to the Bazhin Gap, a broad rift to the left of the summit cliffs, was wide open yet the summit was still a long way from their grasp. English gentleman that he was, Mummery now abandoned his attempt and shepherded his sick porter back down

45

A.F. Mummery.

to their first camp, even though he was still highly animated
and his spirit undiminished by his assault on the face.

During that morning and in the days before, on the way
up, Mummery's abiding concern had been to find the best
possible line of ascent, and he had committed the details of
each section of the route to memory, scanning the way
ahead over and over again, perhaps to ensure that the
descent was made with no unnecessary detours. As if driven
by some inner compulsion he had memorized the terrain
like a jigsaw puzzle, piece by piece, a series of images with
seracs, gullies, rocky outcrops. At the first steep section,
shaped like the bow of a ship, he knew he had to descend
to the left. And he knew, too, that it was best to stick to the
thin snow line until it lost itself in the jumble of crevasses.
How important it is to remember a few points of reference
to prevent you suddenly getting lost on the way up or down
the mountain!

Mummery had practised this kind of mountain craft over a period of many years and every time he climbed he forced himself to visualize the reverse image of the route to safeguard the descent. This precaution had often saved his life, as it did now on Nanga Parbat. How else could he have found his way down again? In spindrift or in the mist, every mountain is like a maze. Mummery knew of a possible route to the summit. Would his strength and stamina have been enough to get there and back again? What if he had been forced into an emergency bivouac out in the open? No, he would never have reached the summit of Nanga the following day; it would have been out of the question.

Instead, the story was to unfold in a different, tragic, way.

Continued snowfall made it impossible for Mummery to launch a second assault up the crest of the rock spur he had already reconnoitred, so he decided to abandon the attempt and instead inspect the Diamir Gap at the very head of the valley. Maybe he intended to traverse the Rakhiot ridge with his two Gurkha companions. He had arranged to meet Collie and Hastings on the north side of the mountain. The two men were to transfer the bulk of the expedition's equipment over three small passes on the Chilas side to the Rakhiot Valley – a journey that involved no great risk. But Mummery never arrived.

Hastings and Collie quickly made their way back to the Diamir Valley. The British authorities mobilized a search party of local men from the surrounding valleys, but they found no sign of Mummery. It will perhaps remain unclear quite where and how this pioneer of mountaineering met his fate. Only one thing is certain: in 1895 the descent from the Diamir Gap was impossible. Was Mummery buried by an avalanche? Did he fall into a crevasse? Or had he indeed made one last attempt on the summit, perhaps via the ramp on the North Face that I was to climb 105 years later? That route would at least have offered Mummery a slim chance of reaching the summit of Nanga Parbat.

47

The northern aspect of Nanga Parbat (the Rakhiot side).

In 1930, Willo Welzenbach, the most experienced ice-climbing specialist of the inter-war years, seized upon Walter Schmidkunz' idea of organizing a Nanga Parbat expedition. Schmidkunz, the editor of the German Alpine Club in Munich, who had purchased the German rights of Mummery's book and translated Mummery's last letters to his wife into German, saw Nanga Parbat as the easiest of the eight-thousanders. Willy Merkl then adopted Welzenbach's plan and, in 1932, led a joint German-American team to 'Nanga'. Merkl wished to attempt the mountain from the Rakhiot side, the side of the mountain to which Mummery was last headed. Willy Merkl considered the Diamir Face to be too dangerous and he knew from Mummery that the South Face was unclimbable. Therein lies the allure of the South or Rupal Face of Nanga Parbat: it is commonly regarded as the most impossible of the big Himalayan walls. In his history of Nanga Parbat, Günter Oskar Dyhrenfurth describes the South-East and

Southern aspect of the massif as one of the highest big walls in the world: '4500 vertical metres, the upper half tremendously steep, with rugged buttresses, steep rock steps and hanging seracs. Even the most optimistic and accomplished climber would have to admit that an attempt on this gigantic face is out of the question.'

As a result, the German-American Expedition of 1932 decided to reconnoitre a potential line of ascent from the Rakhiot Valley. They actually managed to get a fair way up, too, and returned to Base Camp without any losses. On the journey home, however, the American Rand Herron – having survived unscathed the avalanches and other dangers on Nanga – fell to his death from the Chefren Pyramid in Egypt. The Nanga Parbat veterans ascribed the whole thing to Fate, while the local prophets of doom proclaimed that the 'demon' of the mountain had taken him. Merkl remained unimpressed by such fanciful notions and described his fascination with the struggle for the summit thus: 'There is no greater objective. Hard-fought was the struggle, near at hand the longed-for summit. Harder still to bear was the failure and bitter the realization that this huge mountain refused to be subjected to our collective will. Yet merely to have stood amongst the ranks of the battle troops, to have prepared the way to one of the highest of mountaineering objectives, brings joy.' The inherent dangers were described in similarly mystical terms: 'Words cannot convey the sheer size and extent of these ice-clad Himalayan precipices. We saw kilometre-long barricades of ice crashing down with a dreadful thundering noise, hardly able to breathe in the eerie gloom of the thick cloud of ice dust that settled as they fell. Everyone spoke of it as the harbinger of doom: the wrathful God of Nanga had cast the first stone. Were the locals really haunted by such bad omens?' No they were not, but this is how the idealized picture of the struggle was to emerge, a struggle that in popular mythology was to become a clash of the titans. Such fond imaginings were also

The 1934 expedition. (left to right) Front row: Schneider, Welzenbach, Aschenbrenner, Merkl, Consul Kapp, Müllritter, Kuhn; Back row: Bernard, Wieland, Capt. Sangster, Hieronimus, Bechtold.

responsible for the notion of the mountain elevated to the position of a supreme ideal. Climbing Nanga Parbat became a synonym for such values as uncompromising effort, loyalty unto death, comradeship and the idea of the rope as a bond for life. Above all this stood the summit: the Holy Grail and a metaphor for the shared objective.

For Merkl, the solution to the last great problems of the Himalaya required 'different assumptions than those applicable to the conquering of mountains in the Eastern and Western Alps. For there is a difference of whether one has to maintain one's mental and physical powers over a period of days or months. In the Himalaya it is not so much about the power and momentum generated by a tremendous, yet momentary, force of will, as is often crucial for the ascent of the most difficult big faces in the Alps; rather, everything depends upon the ability to hold out, to be constantly prepared to do battle. In the Himalaya, the decisive factor is the cooperation between like-minded characters, the collaborative effort involved that serves only to achieve the big objective rather than one's personal ambition.'

There was one further prejudice that Willy Merkl brought home with him from his first Nanga Parbat trip: the myth that this was the easiest of the eight-thousanders to climb.

'It can be climbed and it can be climbed by our route,' he said; of this he was convinced.

Two years later, in 1934, they were off again, this time with Willo Welzenbach in the team. But why was it that Merkl was again named as the leader of the expedition? It was force of habit, just like in politics, where the leader assumes the lead simply because he has done so before, and also because Merkl was a man well capable of generating enthusiasm. And because he was so sure of victory.

'Do you believe in victory?' a journalist asked the expedition leader before departure.

'Yes,' Merkl replied. 'We must succeed at all costs.'

'And what if you are not successful?'

'Then I won't come home!'

The mountain had no need of such heroics; Merkl, however, needed the mountain. He longed for 'his Nanga' like the addict needs his drugs. Such a mountain is well suited to a hero's death.

The Second Attempt

By 6 July 1934, Schneider, Aschenbrenner, Drexel and Welzenbach were at Camp 4. Alfred Drexel, a big bear of a man, was complaining of headaches. A short while later Drexel decided to descend. He had to get back down to

Silver Saddle, Silver Plateau and Main Summit of Nanga Parbat.

Camp 2 as fast as possible; the headaches were growing steadily worse.

On 7th June Drexel could no longer stand and had to lie down. The expedition doctor arrived from Base Camp. By 8th June Drexel was lying unconscious in his tent. The doctor diagnosed pneumonia; there was bleeding from the lungs. Porters rushed up to the camp with oxygen equipment. On 8th June at 9 o'clock in the evening Drexel died at the camp, the probable cause being acute pulmonary oedema.

Four weeks later, as the others arrived at Camp 7 below the Silver Saddle, six of the Darjeeling porters were suffering from altitude sickness. The camp was at 7100m, too high for them to recover. There was nothing for it; the sick men had to turn back. With a heavy heart, Fritz Bechtold bade farewell to his comrades and led the sick porters back down to Camp 4.

Five climbers and a dozen porters remained for the last, and most difficult, part of the climb – the summit push.

Erwin Schneider and Peter Aschenbrenner, two top-class climbers from the Tyrol, took the lead. They broke trail, the others following in their wake. The lead team reached the Silver Plateau, the great snow plateau beyond the Silver Saddle, and carried on climbing. Ahead lay the virgin summit of the unclimbed mountain. Both men were certain that the following day the ascent of the plateau and the ridge beyond would be possible. The main summit looked to be just a few hours distant, surely it would be no big deal. Up and down again in a day was the best strategy, they reckoned.

Back down at the flat ground of the Silver Plateau they searched around for a place out of the wind to pitch the tents. Camp 8 was established at a height of 7600m. The others soon arrived – three sahibs and more than a dozen porters, far too many people so high on the mountain. But that evening as they sat together the fears began to subside. The weather was good and there was a general mood of confidence that tomorrow the summit would be theirs for the taking.

During the night, however, the wind increased. A storm blew up, the weather grew fierce, and snow battered the tents at Camp 8. The iced-up flysheets had to be held down from the inside to prevent them blowing away. The snowstorm blew tatters of mist before it and lashed masses of new snow into the makeshift shelters. On 7th July the team was stormbound: no let up, no respite, no hope of action. Any sunlight was smothered in the whirling mass of snowflakes. An eerie gloom and the roaring of the storm continued unabated throughout the morning and afternoon. The most experienced members of the team huddled together; they had no idea of what was to come. Merkl, Aschenbrenner, Schneider, Welzenbach and Wieland sat stunned into inactivity.

Merkl advised that they wait it out.

The sahibs and porters remained where they were, lying in their sleeping bags as the hurricane increased in force. Cooking was impossible. They even gave up melting snow. The second night, a night of sinking hope, lasted an eternity. The men simply lay there, throats parched, panting, coughing, miserable. Merkl spoke, attempting to offer some consolation: 'Storms never last long at these altitudes.'

For two long nights the men toughed it out at Camp 8, still hoping for good weather to make their summit bid. But it was all in vain; the storm again increased in force.

On the 8th July, clouds again enveloped the summit. And still there was this wind! Nerves were stretched to breaking point. There was now nothing else for it, they had to turn back, to descend, and still every one of them believed he could return for another attempt after just a few days.

Aschenbrenner, Schneider and two of the porters set off first to prepare the way down. As they left the others were just getting ready to depart. Like shadows, they knelt before the tents, struggling with crampons and rucksacks. When, hours later, the cloud cover parted for a brief moment, Aschenbrenner and Schneider could see Merkl, Wieland, Welzenbach and eight porters high above on the Silver Saddle. They were following them down.

When Schneider and Aschenbrenner finally arrived at Camp 4 they turned around again for a look. They saw nothing. Nevertheless, they thought, the others surely could not be far behind.

The lead team had now reached the safety of the camp. The second group, however, was to abandon their descent before reaching Camp 7. Sahibs and porters became separated, growing further apart in the thick swirling snow. By now almost exhausted, they stumbled downhill, little by little, step by step; it was every man for himself. Onwards and downwards they went, their progress measured at a snail's pace.

For two days now, since their failed attempt to push on to the summit, they had eaten nothing and had been drinking far too little. The wind and the cold were barbaric, their throats were red raw. They continued to descend, climbing down a seemingly endless ridge with huge, tilted slopes of firn snow off to their left, and to the right, nothing but a void. The lower they got the more lethargic and lackadaisical they became. They were moving like zombies. There was no longer any chance of respite. They rested lying down, faces pressed against the snow. The air was cold and keen, cutting into their lungs, yet still they pressed on, lifting one foot in front of the other, stamping the snow, breathing deeply. Then the second foot, placing it a few centimetres lower. They had to force themselves to stay alive, breathing in, breathing out, then taking another step. Like children still learning to walk, the climbers crawled along, every movement leaving them totally spent. Yet still they all believed they would make it; still they dared hope. All of them were now frostbitten and were suffering from bad coughing fits, their voices were weak, but they were no longer really consciously aware of their suffering. Although at a subconscious level they sensed where they were and what a pitiful state their bodies were in, everything now happened as if in a trance. The damage to their respiratory tracts was becoming progressively worse as the ice crystals in the air sliced their way like knives into their lungs. They could not climb down any faster; they no longer wanted to. Men against the mountain, they began to die.

In such a situation one is no longer capable of thought. Between pain and death there is an intermediate stage that is absent in such cases: self reflection. All thoughts and predictions concerning what is to come are simply shut out. All of the usual thought processes that would normally induce us to use past experience to avoid potential threats and dangers in good time somehow go astray.

The ridge snaked away into nothingness. There was no longer any certainty, just the immeasurable greyness and the constant storm. And the cold! All the men were wrapped up in thick clothing but since setting off that morning their body temperature had fallen by stages. Nor was there any shelter to be had from the cutting wind that sliced down from the

Silver Saddle, increasing in strength all the time. They had a few provisions in their rucksacks but to get at them they would have had to take off the rucksack, remove their gloves and undo the sack, all the while perched on a steep slope in the storm. Fearful of losing something or even dropping the rucksack, they decided to wait until they reached a less steep section of the face where they could at least stand in relative safety. So they struggled on, growing colder and colder, getting slower and slower, by now completely apathetic.

Crested waves of wind-blown powder snow whipped across the face, the fierce gusts roaring like crashing surf and rolling down the mountain like avalanches. Clothing stiff with ice, the lenses of their snow goggles encrusted with rime, the men stumbled down the snow slopes. Their feet were numb, their fingers stiff and wooden. Visibility was almost nil. The route – not really a route as such, just a series of indefinite slopes and ridges – seemed to grow more dangerous with every step, but waiting for each other and discussing the options was no longer possible. The instinct for self preservation was stronger than the community spirit. Order was waning; chaos was gaining the upper hand.

Towards 11 o'clock in the morning of the 9th of July the heavy snow clouds parted briefly and for a few minutes the ridge was visible from Camp 4. Great plumes of snow hundreds of metres in length blew from the Silver Saddle, trailing out horizontally above the Rakhiot Face. Between the feature known as the 'Moor's Head' and the Silver Saddle, beneath the left-hand-pinnacle of the Silberzacken, a large party could be seen descending. Viewed from below, it was a ghostly scene.

Had the great tragedy already commenced up there? Yes; Wieland was dead. The porters who had shared an emergency bivouac between Camp 7 and Camp 8 with Merkl and Welzenbach brought the news that Wieland Sahib had simply sat down in the snow and never got up again. Had he fallen asleep? He would not be waking up again now, that

High-altitude porters: Da Thundu, Kikuli, Kitar and Pasang.

much was sure. They, too, had no tent; just a couple of wet sleeping bags and a blanket.

Two days later, at around midday, the men at Camp 4 saw seven or eight people descending the ice wall of Rakhiot Peak. 'At last!' they exclaimed.

Straight away they began to make tea and cook some food; tents were pitched and beds made ready. Bernard, the expedition doctor, prepared his black bag of medicines. Then they set out to meet the descending party.

But now there were only four men wading down through the snow towards them. In a state of near total exhaustion, four porters arrived in camp: the Sherpas Pasang and Da Thundu, Kitar, one of Merkl's personal servants, and Kikuli, Wieland's personal porter. Kikuli fell on the last steep slope before the camp, unable to go any further. The Sherpas were totally spent. Each of them had frostbitten hands and feet. Pasang, who had lost his snow goggles, was snowblind.

Aschenbrenner at Camp 4 after a rescue attempt.

The question 'Where are the three Germans?' was met only with silence. The only information about this huge tragedy was in the reports made by the porters at a later date. The porters' words were as every bit as shocking as their physical state.

Kitar had this to say: 'As we left Camp 8 in the morning of 8th July the sahibs and porters were still in good shape. All of us were. Then, below the Silver Saddle, the sahibs explained that they wished to establish an interim camp, perhaps because they were not able to go any further. We had only three sleeping bags, two for us porters and one for the sahibs. So Welzenbach slept out in the snow with no protection. That evening, although we could not prepare any food, the storm was not as bad as at Camp 8. Even the snow was falling less thickly. In the evening Nima Nurbu died at this interim camp. During the night Merkl's right hand and both of Wieland's hands got badly frostbitten.

'The next morning Welzenbach was in the best shape of all the sahibs. To make the descent to Camp 7 easier he buried the shaft of an ice axe in the snow and anchored the rope to it, which we porters then climbed down. Only Gay-Lay, Angtsering and Dakshi remained at the interim camp; they felt ill and wanted to sit it out for a further night. We had been waiting for more than an hour at Camp 7 when Merkl and Welzenbach arrived. They told us that, due to the cramped sleeping arrangements, we should carry on down to Camp 6.'

Of Wieland they had seen nothing.

Kitar continued: 'Descending a flat ridge, we were sometimes up to our chests in snow. The storm was so dreadful that we were unable to reach Camp 6. We spent the night in a snow hole. The following morning, whilst descending the Rakhiot ice wall, we met Pasang, Nima Dorje and Pinzo Nurbu, who had originally been a day ahead of us but had lost their way in the snow storm. While descending the steep face the storm blew up again with such force that we were rooted to the spot. How could we have carried on down with no strength and zero visibility? Nima Dorje and Nima Tashi died on the ropes on Rakhiot Peak. We managed to get Pinzo Nurbu down as far as Camp 5 where, 3m from the tents, he collapsed and died. We waited for Da Thundu, who had in the meantime untied from the dead men's rope, then we set off together in the direction of Camp 4.'

Long after midnight the Sherpas fell into a disturbed sleep. In their nightmares they walked over corpses, they fell whilst climbing, they lay in the snow, their hands frostbitten, hallucinating, snowblind. They did not know why they were still alive; they did not want to know. The storm wind still whipped across the ice slopes, growing more violent as it swept down from the Silver Saddle. Had Merkl and Welzenbach already reached Camp 6? Would they have been able to locate the tents with visibility down to just a few metres? Without additional oxygen they would not last long up there, for sure. Was Wieland dead?

Down at Camp 4 the tents were still being pummelled by the wind.

When, next morning, they all went out into the storm one of them heard a voice. The Sherpas and sahibs at Camp 4 were in a state of physical and emotional exhaustion, and now, the very thing they had been unable to imagine actually seemed to be happening: maybe they really were still alive up there! It was only the paralysing certainty that they were unable to help that caused them to doubt this.

Nevertheless, they still tried to organize a rescue for Merkl and Welzenbach from Camp 4. Over and over again they tried to get back up the mountain, but it was impossible. Three days passed. After all their attempts to bring help, apathy set in. No one at Camp 4 believed any longer that rescue was possible.

Then, on 13th July, three people were spotted high up on the ridge below Camp 7. They were half-way down to Camp 6. In the gap below the rise to the Moor's Head one of them stepped forward and waved. From time to time a shout was carried down on the wind. Wasn't that the voice of Merkl, the expedition leader? And didn't the shout sound like a distant call for help? Or was it all just an illusion?

The survivors kept staring up at the ridge until they could see no more, until common sense deserted them. Since they could not help they did not want to imagine that their comrades might still be alive. It is only when a state of detachment prevails that such helplessness can be endured. And so they waited, and with the waiting came calm acceptance.

Chapter III

The Death of Willy Merkl

The snow ridge and the summit of Nanga Parbat with the Shoulder (right) and South-East Buttress (left).

For him, the mountain was the highest of holy shrines, a lifetime objective. The mountain, with its myriad rapturous joys, with its bright golden adventures, its manly struggles and austere mortal dangers. It is not for us to cast doubt or to despair of the legitimacy of his actions, to weigh the pros and cons of this bold deed. Heroic greatness lies in the willingness to dedicate oneself body and soul, even unto the end. The value of playing for the highest stakes of all – one's life – lies not in success but in the deed itself.

Karl Maria Herrligkoffer

Willi Merkl, 1934 expedition leader.

Nature had predestined Merkl to be a leader and had also granted him the physical attributes necessary to endure storm and cold right to the very end. One thing is sure: he tasted the deep pain of the tragedy right down to the last bitter dregs. On 9th July he was witness to the death of our beloved Uli Wieland; four days later his friend and trusted climbing partner Willo Welzenbach died next to him in the tent.

Fritz Bechtold

At the end, all that Willy Merkl had left was a rough, harsh blanket. And this for a man who was the leader of the team, the one who had thought of everything, who had considered every necessity. He was forced to endure the pain and grief to the bitter end. Defeat in the fight for the mountain, the abandonment of the objective, the death of his trusty companions and his worthy porters – no one suffered and experienced all this in the same ghastly way he did.

Karl Maria Herrligkoffer

The Tragedy

In a snow hole on the East Ridge of Nanga Parbat, Merkl and Gay Lay still waited. Would their companions come for them? Would they bring tea, food and medicine? Outside, the storm raged unabated.

Down at Camp 4, too, the hurricane still blew. Again and again, they looked up to the ridge. The profile of the East Ridge was clearly visible whenever there was a break in the cloud. Were those figures up there? Was that someone waving, silhouetted against the glowering sky? Then the plumes of snow came again as the wind grew fiercer. But was that not a shout for help that could be heard during a brief pause from the howling of the storm?

The bewildered climbers and their sick porters knew exactly what was to be done. But what could they attempt now that they had not already tried?

The night of the 13th/14th July passed tortuously slowly for Aschenbrenner, Bernard and Schneider at Camp 4. They were full of doubt. Nevertheless, as night gave way to day, they continued their vigil. What were they waiting for? For a miracle to happen. And happen it did, for later that evening one of the missing men returned as if from the dead. He came down from Camp 5 alone, staggering through the storm. Like a ghost, he appeared through the mist then vanished again. With tea and rum, they went to meet him, peeled the thickly encrusted snow from his face and half carried him back down to camp. It was Angtsering, Merkl's second Sherpa. Totally exhausted and suffering terrible frostbite, he had fought his way back down to join the survivors.

Angtsering at Base Camp.

Angtsering looked like a dead man, like one who had returned from Hell. Was he still of sound judgement? No; he bore no news of Bara Sahib, as they called Merkl, not even a word of greeting; no note, no letter. Could it be that Merkl and Gay Lay were still somehow alive up there in their snow hole? Angtsering did not know. His account was to become the basis for the last news item on the death of the two 'heroes'. *It was to fall to Fritz Bechtold to summarize the details of Angtsering's report and to record the events for posterity.*

Angtsering explained: 'Since we had no food I was all for getting down as fast as possible, but Merkl, Bara Sahib, preferred to wait until we could see the people we had already seen once coming up between Camp 4 and Camp 5 and bringing us provisions. Welzenbach died during the night of 13th July. We left the dead sahib, Welzenbach, lying in the tent and set off that same morning for Camp 5. Merkl plodded along

64

alone, supporting himself on two ice axes. Since we were not able to manage the climb back up to the Moor's Head we built a snow cave on the flat col. Bara Sahib and Gay Lay slept together, wrapped up in one of the porter's blankets. I also had a blanket but nothing underneath. On 14th July I stepped out of the cave and shouted loudly for help. As there was nobody to be seen at Camp 4 I suggested to Merkl that we go down. He agreed.'

The question naturally arises as to why Angtsering stayed at the emergency camp below the Silver Saddle with the Sherpas Gay Lay and Dakshi on the morning of 9th July.

Angtsering explained: 'Because we were too exhausted and partially snowblind. We only had two sleeping bags. Dakshi died up there on the second night. While descending to Camp 7 we stumbled upon the body of Wieland, hunched behind a pile of snow. The corpse lay just 30m from the tent.'

At Camp 7 they found Merkl and Welzenbach. They were both still alive.

Angtsering continued: 'First I had to clean out the tent, which was full of snow. This was at Merkl's request. Then we got ourselves ready for the night. Our communal sleeping bag was so encrusted in snow and ice that only Gay Lay could sleep in it. Even the sahibs slept without sleeping bags, just on foam mats.'

The situation was hopeless. There was nothing more to eat. Merkl was still hoping that the others would bring provisions up from the lower camps; but his hopes were in vain. All attempts at rescue foundered in the huge masses of new snow that had fallen. After the death of Drexel, Wieland, Welzenbach and six Sherpas also perished. The porter Gay Lay nevertheless stayed with Merkl, even though he could have saved himself. 'Loyal even unto death', Bechtold was later to write of the Sherpas.

Perhaps the Sherpas in the 1930s really were so faithful and dutiful that they were prepared to die with their sahibs.

Then again, perhaps their death was later accorded such heroic status by the surviving sahibs merely to salve their conscience.

Against all the dictates of common sense, on 15th and 16th July Schneider and Aschenbrenner again set off towards Camp 5, but their attempts were unsuccessful and they ground to a halt in the deep new snow. When the wind came from the direction of the ridge they thought they heard shouts but there was no one to be seen at the Saddle. On 17th July the weather was again bad. By now the men at Camp 4 were desperate, their strength ebbing fast. Those who could do so, set off down the mountain. The shouts from the ridge had stopped.

Willy Merkl and his porter Gay Lay were dead.

The expedition was now at an end and with the news of the tragedy those returning home brought with them those defining emotions that were to turn Nanga Parbat into the 'German Mountain of Destiny'.

Herrligkoffer had this to say: 'Willy Merkl's life as a climber had reached its zenith. What more could there be? The summit – and then? The only thing to do was to establish a new point of reference. There had to be new desire to collect and direct the streams of thought, in any direction. Did this Earth have something greater to offer him, and was this in fact possible? Was there a second task, one which could take possession so completely of every fibre of his being?'

Thus it was that, tacitly and unbidden, an eighteen-year-old German youth took over as heir presumptive to the legacy of the heroes. Merkl's half-brother Karl Maria Herrligkoffer stepped into the role of the dead expedition leader and swore to make Merkl's dream a reality.

Chapter IV

The Legacy

The 'Fairy Meadow' on the Rakhiot side of Nanga Parbat.

It was on 24 July 1934 that I knew for certain that my brother was dead. During the following pain-filled night I made a solemn resolve to place a simple monument to him in the hearts of those who had known him and all the many who had shared so warmly in his life and in his expeditions.

Karl Maria Herrligkoffer

Dr Karl M. Herrligkoffer.

Nanga Parbat will ensure that the memory of the men
left there will never fade away, just as the figures of
the Pharaohs retain unscathed their spiritual wealth
and their serene countenance, even after thousands of
years in the pyramids.

Hermann Schäfer

The objective shines like a beacon above Merkl's
grave, calling the younger generation of mountaineers
to new action... to this battle for Nanga Parbat. It is
Merkl, too, who mobilizes the German forces to
mount a fresh assault on the mountain, in order that
the death and the pioneering work of the four heroes
might not have been in vain.

Karl Maria Herrligkoffer

Herrligkoffer's Obsession

Willy Merkl was dead. But his half-brother Karl Maria Herrligkoffer had made it his lifetime's objective to keep his memory alive: 'Now he rests forever in the bright light of the eternal snows of the mountain for which he struggled so hard and which, in the end, was too strong an adversary for him. The struggle for the summit, however, continues.' Herrligkoffer now took on the legacy of his brother. He, too, wished to fight and to lead and, in the end, to be stronger than the mountain. And so he decided to become a climber and to organize an expedition. Overnight, he had taken his brother's mountain and made it his own.

Herrligkoffer again: 'Such tragedy! In his last hours Willy Merkl had nothing more than a single Sherpa's blanket, which he shared with his trusty porter Gay Lay.'

Did all this hero worship for his brother also conceal the willingness to die a hero's death himself? The young Herrligkoffer daydreamed about his mountain, his expedition team, his heroism – of the joy and the tragedy of being Merkl's brother.

When, in 1938, the bodies of Merkl and Gay Lay were found on the Moor's Head it became clear that the Sherpa had died at his master's side. This fact, this willingness to sacrifice oneself – the Sherpa dying with his sahib on the ridge up to the Silver Saddle – was glorified, held up as proof of the loyalty of the Sherpas. This idea of loyalty unto death became a part of the National Socialist doctrine and of mountaineering ideology. It was exactly this kind of unquestioning loyalty, together with the ideas of comradeship and the principle of the leader, that Herrligkoffer inherited from Merkl.

'Throughout his life and in every situation Willy Merkl had always been a good comrade; indeed, one of the best. In his last hours he was to receive a declaration of comradeship the like of which had never before been made in the history of the Himalaya. Gay Lay, who, together with Angtsering, might perhaps have still been able to save himself, stayed with his Bara Sahib and remained faithful to him even unto death,' said Herrligkoffer.

Although Herrligkoffer lacked the ability and the experience required to be a great mountaineer, he had internalized his brother's climbs to such an extent that he felt himself drawn to make the journey to 'Nanga'. Every time he was out hill walking he dreamed of his mountain, of Nanga Parbat. That is where he wanted to go; that is where he felt compelled to go. Although all this yearning caused him somehow to forget to become a mountaineer himself, he wanted to go right to the top. And so, gradually, a plan began to form in his mind, a plan for a Nanga Parbat expedition, which he would put together and dedicate to the memory of Willi Merkl. In 1952 he was ready. Herrligkoffer was by now 36 years old and a general practitioner. It never occurred to him to question why it was that all six pre-war expeditions to Nanga Parbat had failed. In his opinion, the experienced expedition leaders and the many top climbers who had failed on the mountain after Merkl had simply not shared Merkl's vision. Perhaps it was also down to the cruel hand of Fate that seemed to hang over every endeavour on the Naked Mountain, exerting a magical power of attraction over those who dreamed of success. Herrligkoffer wished to break that spell.

Herligkoffer planned his expedition for 1953. His intention was to tackle the eight-thousander with an Austro-German team of climbers via the Rakhiot Face, just as his brother had done. He wanted to do everything in exactly the same way as Willy Merkl: the same face of the mountain, the same route and the same strategy. The Tyrolean Aschenbrenner was to

After the 1934 tragedy: Schneider, Aschenbrenner, Bechtold and Müllritter at Base Camp.

be on the team again, one of the climbers who had survived in 1934 and the man who had gone higher on Nanga Parbat than any other.

Meanwhile another Tyrolean, an ambitious climber similarly obsessed by mountains and mountaineering but, unlike the starry-eyed idealist Herrligkoffer, a man not prone to such flights of fantasy, was following the expedition's preparations in the media with keen interest. His name was Hermann Buhl, he lived in Innsbruck and he was the best climber of the time.

So Dr Karl Maria Herrligkoffer wanted to lead an expedition to Nanga Parbat in the summer of 1953, Buhl thought, as he asked himself how in the world he might be allowed to participate. He was prepared to give of his time, his skills and his passion for the expedition and for the 'summit victory'.

Despite this, Buhl remained sceptical, for Herrligkoffer was an unknown name in mountaineering circles. He was totally inexperienced, yet quite obviously a master of the art of propaganda. Many newspapers published his plans and requests for donations.

Buhl, at the time a self-assured, obsessive and extraordinarily ambitious young man, knew that he was one of the best climbers in the German-speaking countries, and one of the best in the world – and he wanted more. That is why he had to go to Nanga Parbat, to show what he was really capable of. What elite climber would not have wanted the chance to prove himself on the highest of all objectives? But how could Buhl join the Herrligkoffer expedition? No one had spoken to him about it, he could only wait. Finally, to his relief, the magic telegram arrived, the invitation to join the expedition. It brought a complete change in Hermann Buhl's life.

'The telegram came as a big surprise to me. The thing I had no longer dared hope for had actually happened: they were asking me to participate in the expedition. Full of enthusiasm, I agreed and immediately threw myself heart and soul into the preparations. I was in the expedition office almost every day, helping with the packing, organizing and paperwork,' Buhl commented.

Buhl no longer questioned who this Dr Herrligkoffer was or what his mountaineering credentials might be. For him, Herrligkoffer was the man who was giving him the opportunity to go to the Himalaya. In any case, Herrligkoffer had also promised that he would only be leading the expedition as far as Base Camp; on the mountain itself, Peter Aschenbrenner was to be in charge of strategy. In other words, there were to be two expedition leaders, one low down and one higher up the mountain, and Buhl wanted to be high up, as high as he could go. But many Himalayan veterans continued to view the Herrligkoffer expedition with scepticism, in particular Paul Bauer, a Munich man who had led half a dozen Himalayan expeditions. Now too old to organize another such enterprise himself, Bauer became a vehement critic of Herrligkoffer's plans. Yet this only fuelled the naive dreamer's obsession. And Herrligkoffer also had influential contacts in the world of politics and finance. Undeterred, he remained doggedly committed to his purpose.

Buhl: 'With the benefit of the documents left by his half brother, Dr Herrligkoffer was now able to draw up his expedition plan. At times we were concerned that this might turn into a mammoth undertaking and we did try to put the brakes on, but Herrligkoffer would not allow us to interfere in anything and worked away at his project with an iron will.'

It seemed as if nothing could stop the man. Criticism and concerns fell on deaf ears, scornful jibes were simply ignored. Herrligkoffer stuck doggedly to his plans and said 'The defining moment for me was certainly the death of my half brother Willy Merkl.' To be sure, whenever anyone wants to go all the way to the summit of Nanga Parbat a certain degree of fanaticism is a prerequisite for success. But why was it that a hill walker with no chance of reaching the summit could work himself up into such a state over an expedition to an eight thousander? Where did this stubbornness, this naivety, come from?

'German climbers must achieve Merkl's objective,' was Herrligkoffer's reply. And it fell to him, Merkl's brother, to lead the German climbers to Nanga Parbat. The fact that Hermann Buhl was an Austrian was immaterial; Herrligkoffer had never considered Austria as being a foreign country.

The 1953 team was a good one. Although the individual members hardly knew each other they would complement each other well. Herrligkoffer had engaged his men to do specific jobs; some would stay at Base Camp, while others were earmarked for the summit push. The renowned film maker Hans Ertl, who had flown in from South America to join them, was to make a documentary of the expedition.

Although Ertl, 'the vagabond' and Buhl, the top climber, had the reputation of being difficult, they slotted smoothly into the team during the preparatory phase. On the mountain, too, there were at first no problems with the two men. On the contrary, they were the driving force of the expedition and the ones on whom all hopes rested. However, Buhl and Ertl were by nature solitary performers.

The Austro-German Willi Merkl Memorial Expedition. (left to right): Dr Frauenberger, Ertl, Rainer, Köllensperger, Aschenbrenner, Kempter, Dr Herrligkoffer, Aumann, Bitterling, Buhl.

'Hans Ertl really showed himself to advantage during the expedition. He was a good companion, helpful and friendly. From time to time he even brought breakfast to our tents,' Herrligkoffer commented.

The German and Austrian climbers, with Peter Aschenbrenner, Hermann Buhl and Kuno Rainer representing the Tyrol, reached the Fairy Meadow and established Base Camp a little further up, on the great Rakhiot moraine below the North-East Face.

This expedition was similarly plagued by sudden falls in temperature and a lot of snow, which threatened to foil their summit attempt. The expedition leaders had already ordered the climbers back to Base as Buhl was gathering his last ounces of strength for his solo summit bid.

Many difficult days lay behind him but Buhl carried on breaking trail, past the Moor's Head, the last resting place of Willy Merkl, climbing on to the deep notch between Rakhiot Peak and the Silver Saddle, where the last camp was to have been sited. The Munich man Otto Kempter and four of the

74

porters followed. Ertl and Frauenberger stayed behind at the Moor's Head. Although they were in fine form, they intended to wait for the porters to return, descend with them to Camp 4 and head back up the following day. There was only room enough for two at the assault camp, Buhl and Kempter.

Camp 5. The little storm tent was soon pitched. Above lay the ridge leading to the Silver Saddle, glowing in the evening light. To the left, the South Face fell away sharply to the Rupal Valley; to the right, a diffuse violet light played over the glaciers. There were still more than 1200m of vertical height and 6km to go to the summit. By the time they had cooked a meal and filled the water bottles it was 10 o'clock in the evening. The wind was blowing up. Would the tent hold out? Unable to sleep, Buhl crawled outside and used ski poles and ice axes to anchor the tent a second time. Around midnight, the wind dropped slightly. Buhl was deep in thought, already preoccupied with his summit bid. Glancing at the time, he was pleased to see that it was 1 o'clock – time to get up and get moving.

It was the 3rd of July, 1953.

Buhl's Solo Climb

Hermann Buhl was well acquainted with the diaries of the previous expeditions but it was the words of his fellow Tyroleans that he trusted above all. He intended to set off alone and very early, since the last camp was a long way down and he knew that the German, Otto Kempter, was too slow to keep pace with him. Buhl wanted to move fast and allow plenty of time to get to the summit and back again in one day.

Otto Kempter was still lying in his sleeping bag as Buhl brewed tea, got dressed, packed his rucksack and stepped out into the snow.

Hermann Buhl on the East Ridge of Nanga Parbat.

Outside, the wind had dropped, there was a bright moon and it was not too cold – ideal conditions for a summit push. After all, hadn't Hans Ertl, a veteran of many expeditions and a man with enough experience to assess the potential dangers of a solo bid, encouraged Buhl to go it alone? Ertl had boosted Buhl's self confidence. The day before, when Buhl had gone against the express wishes of the expedition leadership and announced his decision to go should the weather be good enough, Ertl had backed him up. After Aschenbrenner had threatened to leave the expedition if a summit attempt were made, Herrligkoffer had completely lost control of things.

Buhl was now making rapid progress. The men high up on the mountain were now in the hands of Fate. What else should Buhl have done? At times like these, everyone did whatever seemed right to them.

Ertl explains: 'During those decisive days – at the end of June and beginning of July 1953 – when I rebelled against the often-repeated order from Herrligkoffer to retreat back to Base and, as the most experienced member of the expedition, simply took it upon myself to seize the initiative and press for a summit attempt, I did so primarily because of the pressure to succeed that I, as a professional cameraman, felt.'

In Buhl, Ertl saw a chance that the summit might indeed be reached. He wanted success and he wanted a good film in the can to take home with them.

On 3 July 1953 Buhl set out from a tiny, ice-encrusted tent at 6900m. It was now two hours past midnight. What this little man had in mind was inconceivable. It was the act of a man obsessed by an idea in the face of almost certain death; a monstrous undertaking, seemingly contrary to all mountaineering logic and all possibility of success.

Buhl passed beneath huge cornices and climbed a steep snow rib to join the ridge. The sky was still clear and starry, the moon shone brightly and there was virtually no wind. The snow was wind blown and hard packed. Buhl strapped his crampons on. Below and to his right the snow slopes fell away sharply, broken by steeper bands of ice; to the left of the ridge the view was of a bottomless void.

At the start of the traverse to the Silver Saddle Buhl took a short rest. It was 5 o'clock. The sun was rising behind the Karakorum, and he could make out the dark silhouette of K2, then Masherbrum, Rakaposhi and the Mustagh Tower. Two hours later he was standing at the Silver Saddle. Ahead lay the great snow plateau, 3km in length, flat at first then rising gently before the steep climb to the fore-summit. The altimeter showed 7400m. There was a vertical gain of a further 500m to the horizon. The snow was hard packed and sculpted by the wind into deep striations. With every step progress became more and more strenuous. Buhl could feel the air growing thinner. The snowfield stretched endlessly before him.

Otto Kempter, lagging far behind, was later forced to give up right here, at the Silver Saddle. Meanwhile, Buhl struggled on towards the fore-summit, each step now measured in centimetres. The climbing was no longer a fun thing; it was pure hard graft. First there were the cramped conditions in the last camp

Rakhiot Peak and the ridge leading to the Silver Saddle.

and now this unutterable torture that grew worse with every step. The question now was how much more pain Buhl could endure.

The lone climber felt numb. Despite having to concentrate extremely hard he was emotionally drained, dull and listless. The blood pounded in his head. What a difference this was to life down in the valley! Screwing his eyes up into tiny slits, he looked out over the barren expanse of snow and saw nothing, just brightness and the dark sky above, a mono-chrome landscape bled dry of all colour. He was seized by a feeling of terrible isolation. He had never been slower, or felt weaker or more exhausted than now.

Where the slope steepened towards the fore-summit, Buhl decided to leave his rucksack behind. Stuffing his Tyrolean pennant, his gloves, a flask of Bolivian coca tea and some Pervitin and Padutin into his pockets, he tied his anorak around his waist and continued his climb, ice axe in hand. It was now 2 o'clock in the afternoon and there were still 300m of vertical gain before the summit. Would he be able to summon the energy to continue? How long could he keep going? In the Alps, 300m of ascent are nothing remarkable; at an altitude of 8000m it is like a mountain in itself. A steep, heavily corniced rock ridge lay ahead. Buhl took two Pervitin tablets. Then he worked his way up from one rise to the next, turning a rock gendarme by an awkward hand traverse and climbing an overhanging, 10m wall.

At 6 o'clock in the evening he finally stood at the Shoulder at 8060m. Strength ebbing fast now, he forced himself to go on. He drank his last mouthful of coca tea and traversed across to the north side. He was now crawling on all fours. Finally, he noticed that the ground was no longer rising. Seventeen hours after leaving his tent, he had reached the highest point. Buhl later admitted that he did not realize the significance of that moment. He was just pleased to be up there and relieved that the torture was over, temporarily at least. He was a shadow of his former self.

Moving as if in a trance, he took the pennant, the Tyrolean flag, from his anorak pocket, tied it to his ice axe and took a photograph. It was now noticeably colder.

Buhl stayed up there for a while, on the summit of Nanga Parbat, and had a good look around. Behind him lay the Diamir Flank, below and to his right was the Rupal Face, ahead of him the Silver Plateau. There was hardly a breath of wind. The valleys below were black and gloomy. As he gazed down into the immeasurable depths, he felt strangely detached. The world beneath his feet was nothing but a huge black void.

It was now growing dark on the summit, but Buhl stayed perfectly calm. There was no outpouring of emotion, no feeling of pride, nothing. He did not have the strength to be happy, and for the time being lacked the courage to think about the descent. He thought only about the hours that had passed since he had last been able to sleep or even rest. He had hardly eaten a thing in the last few days and now he was suffering from coughing fits, he felt sick and noticed that he was short of breath and he was tortured by cold and exhaustion.

Buhl had no rational explanation for his state of mind. He was so alone, so far away. Thrown into this inhuman world, he suspected that he had been pursuing an illusion, or worse still an insane delusion that had forced him into this situation. But right now he was incapable of giving much thought to the reasons, the origins or the future consequences of such borderline actions. He did not really want to think at all. All he wanted to do now was go down, back to the others.

As he scrambled back down along the summit ridge and the icy cold air penetrated his maltreated lungs, the agony relented. It was as if the mere act of descending were in itself responsible for this new lightness of mood, this feeling of release. At the same time, it must be said, he had the feeling that what was happening was somehow not real. He felt somehow detached from reality, as if he had just awoken from an anaesthetic. Again and again, he heard himself voicing his thoughts out loud, telling himself that it was easier off to the left than keeping to the ridge; that it was now just a question of survival; that he must not allow himself to put a foot wrong; that he must not stumble, not in the state he was in.

From the Shoulder he descended to the west, the wrong direction, and had to climb down an almost vertical rock step. Everything happened as if in a trance.

With no ice axe – he had left it stuck in the snow on the summit – he had only the two ski sticks he had recovered from somewhere near the Shoulder for support. One of his crampons had worked loose. Buhl left it as it was. As night fell, he was still at about 8000m but in the dark it was too dangerous to continue his descent. He could not stay where he was, so he began to search for a place to bivouac. Eventually he found a platform with a loose block big enough to stand on with both feet but with no room to sit down. He had no emergency bivouac gear for a night out in the open, neither sleeping bag nor bivi bag, no rope, not even a rucksack. Holding on with his right hand, he leaned against the block and waited out the night. Midnight came. Buhl nodded off,

The descent from the Silver Saddle.

but only briefly; fear tore him from his slumber. He was racked by repeated shivering fits, his feet frozen and devoid of feeling. 'When the moon comes out I'll carry on down,' he told himself. It provided some small consolation.

At four in the morning on 4th July Buhl continued his epic descent. Climbing down over snowfields and slabs, he reached a gully which ended abruptly in a 10m overhanging cliff. Buhl later said he did not know how he managed to reverse this difficult piece of climbing. But manage it he did and midday saw him back at the rocks in the Diamir Gap, where he fell asleep in the warm sun. But not for long – thirst soon woke him. Totally parched by now, he was starting to hallucinate. He heard voices but there was no one there. Wrapped up in his own obscure, contradictory version of reality, Buhl carried on down the mountain. Did the voices he had heard come from within himself? Or were they symptoms of altitude-induced schizophrenia? He could find no simple explanation for the phenomena that were playing these tricks on him, the figures that accompanied him or the markers pointing the way down. He did not think his reasoning was in any way impaired. He saw ghostly companions, tracks in the snow and stones piled into cairns that showed him the way.

Hermann Buhl had now been close to complete exhaustion for many hours. He was so drained that he was slavering, he could not swallow, could not speak, could not even call for help. Blood and spittle dripped from his mouth and nose. Crazed with thirst, he staggered down the vast, wind-blown snow slopes of the Plateau. Then this lone survivor suddenly spied two dark points moving on the Silver Saddle. He heard voices, too. Were they calling his name, 'Hermann'? 'They are coming to get me,' he thought. But when he approached the Saddle the disappointment was bitter: there was no one there.

Buhl was now taking more and more frequent rests and his steps were becoming shorter and shorter. At the Silver Saddle, he again took the amphetamine Pervitin, but he had no reserves of energy left for the drug to liberate.

At five thirty Buhl was standing on the Silver Saddle, looking down into the valley. The camps looked empty and abandoned. But then, on the Moor's Head, he was able to pick out two figures. It was the others, he thought. Much lighter of step than before, Buhl descended the ridge from the Saddle towards them. Soon afterwards he fell into the arms of Walter Frauenberger and Hans Ertl. Their joy was indescribable but, too hoarse at first to utter a word, Buhl merely croaked like an animal.

The three men spent the night in the little assault tent. Buhl talked and talked, pouring out his story of his solo climb to the summit. He spoke of the hardship, of the difficult ridge leading to the Shoulder, of the bivouac and the hallucinations he had suffered during the descent. It was only now that he was safe and amongst friends that he truly realized he had climbed Nanga Parbat and that an old German mountaineer's dream had now been fulfilled – by him and him alone.

Chapter V

Hermann Buhl's Fury

The view east from the summit, with the Silver Saddle on the left.

We thought there was something a bit odd about all the complicated legal clauses in the expedition contract we were asked to sign, but our expedition leader reassured us that it was a mere formality; that the whole enterprise rested on comradeship and that the exclusive aim of the expedition was to fulfil a sacred legacy.

Hermann Buhl

On the summit of Nanga Parbat.

The first seven-thousander to be climbed was Trisul (7120m), in 1907. 1950 saw the first ascent of an eight-thousander, Annapurna I (8091m). In 1953 Edmund Hillary and Tenzing Norgay stood on the summit of Mount Everest (8848m).

Günther Oskar Dyhrenfurth

The day came when Providence called a halt to the powers of nature and allowed thirteen days of silk and satin to dawn on Nanga Parbat, days and nights when neither storm, nor wind, nor breath of breeze disturbed the ether and no flake of snow danced in the air. And Providence provided, too, three men, of whom one was the heart, the other the head and the third the fist, a fist of steel, hard and unwavering, and allowed them to take the summit that reigned so mightily above us.

Paul Bauer

The summit climb still seems unreal to me. It is like a dream that one cannot explain – so intangible and yet so real.

Hermann Buhl

Return and Isolation

Hermann Buhl set off on his summit bid a highly fit 28-year old, full of wistful yearning. When he returned he had aged 40 years and was completely drained. Deep lines of exhaustion scored his face, his lips were split, his gait clumsy and slow. He had been badly marked by the altitude and the sun. Exhausted, in need of sleep and strung out, a combination of the effort, altitude and amphetamines, he dragged himself back to the camp, supported by Ertl and Frauenberger. Buhl was close to collapse – the victor or the vanquished? His feet were swollen and painful, his racing brain haunted by crazed delusions.

The men took two days to reach Base Camp – their version of civilization – on the green swathe at the foot of the Naked Mountain. With every step that the exhausted Buhl took, it became increasingly apparent that the climb had taken all of his reserves of energy. He was suffering badly, but Buhl did not ask for sympathy; even back at Base Camp he remained silent and subdued.

Hermann Buhl wanted only to rest. And, above all, he wished to return to normal life, to his family and to Innsbruck, as soon as possible.

The three men from the top camp who had 'failed to obey orders' felt ostracized by those at Base Camp. Even the reception was distinctly frosty. Herrligkoffer was dismissive. Buhl himself was treated with disdain; it was as if he had done something wrong. Perhaps the expedition leader felt insulted? At any rate, he made it plain how unimportant Buhl's success was for him and quite openly attempted to exclude Buhl from the group. Was this all down to jealousy? No; the way Herrligkoffer saw it, Merkl's objective had not been achieved. The only thing that counted was the common effort. Buhl had acted alone. And since Buhl's return it had

Hermann Buhl after his return to Base Camp.

become clear to Herrligkoffer that he himself had not stood on the summit; he was just a part of it. To be sure, without his preparatory work Buhl's summit push would never have been possible but, for Herrligkoffer, Merkl's bequest had been about much more. Perhaps Herrligkoffer felt that he had been deceived, robbed of the essential ideal of the enterprise? For Merkl, it had all been about climbing the mountain together – communal victory or communal death.

Back at Base Camp, there were no victory celebrations. What was the point? The food had all been packed away; the summit team dined on scraps. Only the Hunza porters seemed to appreciate Buhl's achievement and draped garlands of flowers around his neck.

The common ideal had disintegrated. Aschenbrenner had already left, perhaps because Buhl had managed to do what he himself had failed to achieve.

On the journey home the members of the expedition were at loggerheads; some were for Herrligkoffer, the others against

Expedition leader and doctor:
Dr Karl M. Herrligkoffer.

him. Why was this? Well, there are several ways of looking at what happened, but Herrligkoffer insisted on his version of events and pointed to the expedition contract, which was originally meant to be a mere formality. Although this meant that the expedition leader was again firmly in charge of proceedings – it was he, and he alone, who was to decide who, where and what was allowed to be published – tensions were growing in the team. Herrligkoffer saw himself as the sole spokesperson of the expedition and he reserved the right to evaluate and exploit the communal success as he saw fit.

For Hermann Buhl the homeward journey was a torment. His frostbitten feet hurt him terribly, but more painful still was the realization that he was being deliberately excluded from Herrligkoffer's plans for a new expedition. Equipment was to be left in Pakistan for a trip to Broad Peak, but Buhl was no longer part of the equation.

A short time later Herrligkoffer publicly announced his triumph. He wanted to tell the whole world that it was his success, that it was only thanks to Merkl and his brother that a self-willed man possessed of supreme skill and ability had been given the chance to achieve something – on their mountain and on their route – that no one had even thought of before, let alone dared to attempt. Buhl's summit push was no longer of any interest to Herrligkoffer; it merely represented one single piece of the communal jigsaw, a natural part of the team's success which Herrligkoffer wished to exploit. It was the victory over the mountain, the mountain that rightly belonged to him and Merkl that he wanted to see celebrated. As long as he presented the summit success – an achievement that was unsurpassed in mountaineering terms – as a small part of his overall expedition strategy, Herrligkoffer would be able to claim it as his own. After all, where would Buhl have been without him? And what would he himself be without the ideals he had inherited from his brother Willy Merkl?

Buhl wrote later: 'Days later, as I was lying in front of my tent at Base Camp at the foot of the mountain, attending to my wounded foot, I often looked up to the two pinnacles 4000m higher, behind which I know the high firn to be, rising up to the sky like a white ribbon, and I let the hours I spent up there pass through my mind's eye. The summit climb still seems unreal to me. It is like a dream, a dream that one cannot explain – so intangible and yet so real.'

Later, at a press conference in Lahore in the presence of the German Ambassador Herr Knips, when talk turned to the summit climb, Buhl attempted to correct a mistake in Herrligkoffer's report and was rudely silenced.

Herrligkoffer's strategy was to come undone. The expedition split into two distinct groups: those who had 'sacrificed personal ambition for communal success' and were to be included on the next Herrligkoffer expedition and those 'who had refused to obey orders' – Ertl, Buhl and Frauenberger.

Dyhrenfurth had this to say: 'When such a peaceable man and one so moderate in his judgements as the magistrate Dr

Frauenberger deems it necessary to contradict Dr Herrligkoffer over the matter of the latter's qualities as an expedition leader, it requires no further comment. It proves that the cooperation did not work.'

The Trick with the Rhetorical 'We'

Back in Munich, Herrligkoffer spoke at length about his expedition. Through press conferences, lectures and interviews he brought news of the communal success to the masses. Herrligkoffer published reports, an expedition diary, a volume of photographs and an 'official book' of the 'summit victory'. Whenever he spoke or wrote he almost always used the 'I' or 'we' forms and in this way, he stylized himself as a mountaineer, a Himalayan summitteer, a hero.

Buhl commented: 'It is important to note that when he writes in the first person singular he was often involved himself. On the other hand, whenever he uses the plural 'we' he was hardly ever there!'

This 'we' device was important for Herrligkoffer, both as a clear message to the outside world and as an internalized feeling. The feeling conjured up by the use of the rhetorical 'we' was not only designed to help the author to participate, at least retrospectively, in the summit assault; it also suggested to the reader that spirit of comradeship that for Merkl and Herrligkoffer were such an indispensable element of any Himalayan expedition. And not least, it served to give the Herrligkoffer faithful the impression that Buhl had really only stood on their shoulders in order to do what he had done.

By denigrating Buhl's solo climb as the selfish act of a loner and a free agent, the expedition leader inflated the importance of the part played by the 'ground troops' and emphasized their willingness to sacrifice personal ambition for the common good of the enterprise as a whole, portraying it as an exemplary team achievement. In mountaineering circles at least, he succeeded in creating an atmosphere of confusion. Hermann Buhl did not recognize himself or his remarkable climb in Herrligkoffer's official expedition report. Although he was well aware that memory is sometimes fallible – which is something that plagues us all – he also knew that facts were facts.

Buhl: 'The closer the reader of the Herrligkoffer book gets to the point at which the summit is reached, the more confusing and unclear the account becomes. The author keeps quiet about a lot of things, while other details are distorted and facts are twisted to produce an expedition story that reflects his own judgement of events.'

What really made Hermann Buhl furious, however, was the way that Herrligkoffer, with the benefit of hindsight, also distorted the one decision that was to become the pre-condition for the collective success of the expedition and therefore for Herligkoffer's own personal success.

Buhl: 'Herrligkoffer neglected to mention that we, the lead team – Ertl, Frauenberger, Kempter and I – were left high and dry; that we were cut off from the team below; that we were refused the support we needed and that the others purposely sat at Base Camp and did nothing while I made my way alone to the summit.'

Instead, there is much talk in Herrligkoffer's reports of the comradeship, of Merkl's legacy, of the 'battle', the 'victory' and other wholesome 'German virtues'. Hermann Buhl could only stomach so much pathos. He gave a series of lectures, penned his own expedition report together with his ghost writer Kurt Maix and then retreated into a kind of inner exile.

Chapter VI

The Mountain and Its Shadow

Chogolisa in the Karakorum, where Buhl died in 1957.

Whenever Dr Karl Maria Herrligkoffer sets off for the far-away Himalaya, for him the journey is like a 'pilgrimage of the heart'. In the land of the highest mountains on Earth, he follows the 'voice of the absolute' and the 'call of the spirit of the world'. The sight of an eight-thousander is described by the Munich doctor as 'probably the strongest of all purely male experiences'.

Der Spiegel

Hermann Buhl

To date, the mountain has claimed thirty-three victims. One of the first was Willy Merkl, my half brother. He perished on the East Ridge. His death was like a legacy for me. In 1953 I led my first expedition to the unconquered mountain giant. And following the same route that had defeated Willy Merkl, the Innsbruck man Hermann Buhl reached the summit in a magnificent solo climb. From here, the gaze roams far away to the distant Karakorum Range with its famous peaks. On the far right is Chogolisa, where in 1957 Hermann Buhl fell to his death through a cornice.

Karl Maria Herrligkoffer

Hermann Buhl, who had stood on the summit of two eight-thousanders, found a mountaineer's grave on the ice face of Chogolisa ... a grave such as my brother Willy Merkl had found at the Moor's Head on Nanga Parbat in 1934. But the battle for the eight-thousanders goes on...

Karl Maria Herrligkoffer

Nanga Parbat as Therapy

After the success on his 'Nanga', Karl Maria Herrligkoffer remained a man obsessed, driven by his inner compulsion – a man in turmoil, at odds with himself. He was not only greedy for success; he wanted recognition. Although he had succeeded in leading a team that placed a man on the summit, he had not stood right at the top himself. What was it that had caused all the expedition leaders before him to fail? Merkl's ideals were higher, of course, and so he, Herligkoffer, must fulfil them. The only question was – how? By stepping out of the human world and into the pure new world beyond the snowline, that was how. And to do that he had to go back to the Himalaya, or at least the Karakorum. Could it even be that Buhl had not been right to the top? The ice axe he had left up there was no proof until someone else found it.

Even as he was bidding farewell to his mountain, Herrligkoffer knew that he would return.

Herrligkoffer: 'I was searching for the path across the piles of debris and scree slopes, gazing in awe at the snow and ice cliffs of this eight-thousander in all their purity and splendour, when I had the feeling that here, at 4000m, I was still strolling amongst earthly things and that it was only up there on the pure snows of this giant mountain that godly greatness was revealed. I thought of my brother.'

As Merkl's representative it had fallen to Herrligkoffer to 'conquer' the summit of Nanga Parbat in his brother's name, but he felt no satisfaction. For who was who in this 'battle'? What was his role? What did his name mean in the 'struggle for the mountain'? He did not know, but still he named icefields, gullies and routes after the dead men, invoking their spirits and keeping the ethics of his brother very much alive.

Meanwhile, what Buhl wanted was due recognition for his solo achievement and a new chance. He knew very well that

A small expedition on the way to Broad Peak.

without him Herligkoffer, even as expedition leader, would
have failed, his name consigned forever to obscurity.

On the mountain, Buhl and Herrligkoffer complemented
each other perfectly. Now, after the event, they stood in each
other's way. Unsure of their own identities, both men set off
again, this time to Broad Peak, although they went their separate ways. Perhaps, after tackling Nanga Parbat together,
they were looking for certainty, or for confirmation of their
elite status? Herligkoffer's 1954 attempt failed. Buhl went to
Broad Peak in 1957. The answers to the questions could be
found in their choice of challenges and each man got what
he deserved. Herrligkoffer continued to follow the catalogue
of values prescribed by his brother – and failed. Buhl adopted a new style – and was successful. When Buhl set off for
Pakistan in 1957 he was thirty-two years old and the father
of three girls. His objective was the summit of Broad Peak in
the Karakorum, the mountain that Herrligkoffer had failed

to climb, an 8047m colossus whose summit ridge topped the 8000m mark at several places along its length. On the second attempt, all four expedition members reached the main summit. Buhl was the last man to top out. And since this tireless man had to prove that he was the toughest of all, he had planned an encore: the ascent of the seven-thousander Chogolisa, without a support team, without pre-prepared camps – with only his partner, Kurt Diemberger.

When Hermann Buhl set off for the summit of Chogolisa after bagging his second eight-thousander he was at the highpoint of his climbing life. But his luck was running out. Did he not know that the shadow of Nanga Parbat lay upon him? The two men did not reach the summit. During the descent, in thick wind-blown snow, Buhl lagged behind. Finally, he lost all sense of direction and met a lonely end, falling to his death when a cornice collapsed. His body was never found.

Nanga Parbat as a Daydream

Meanwhile, two young lads who had grown up in a large family in the South Tyrol were forging a partnership. They were brothers but otherwise had little in common.

I was thirteen, my brother Günther twelve years old.

'As children we did not like each other. Reinhold and I were so different,' Günther later recalled. At the end of June 1957, however, all this was to change when a cruel injustice threw us together as accomplices united against the rest of the world. At home in South Tyrol, I found my younger brother Günther cowering in a dog kennel. Our father, during one of his fits of rage, had thrashed Günther so badly with the dog whip that he could no longer walk.

On that day we not only became friends; Günther also became my climbing partner and soon he was climbing just as well as I was. We began to talk about trips out together and started to view our climbs as little escapes. We wanted to get away, away from our authoritarian father and away from the injustices of this world. Our climbing soon took on a new dimension.

After the death of Hermann Buhl we both dreamed the same dreams: of Buhl's first ascents, of his style, of a life far, faraway. And of Nanga Parbat, too. We had grown to detest authority in any form, loathed injustice and found middle-class life a torment. The distant mountains became a means of fleeing to an as yet unknown future.

A few years later Günther and I found ourselves beneath our first big rock face in the Dolomites. We were on home ground, in the magnificent rock arena of the Geislerspitzen. At first, we just looked at each other, then back up at the cliff again, as if we could not grasp the fact that, in his youth, our father had tried unsuccessfully to climb this North Face. At that moment, his attempt and subsequent retreat seemed to us a pioneering act. In fact, in our eyes our father was not a real climber at all.

The cliff stood, steep and wet, before us and, climbing as a team rather than as brothers, we did the North Face of the Sass Rigais; 800m of vertical rock, gullies, cracks and, right at the end, 800m of exposure. We had stonefall, and rushing waterfalls, too, and like two tiny characters on a canvas we hung on that tremendous wall, climbing a series of filigreed rock towers with fear our occasional companion. Reaching the summit ridge, we told each other it had been fun.

As climbers, we not only learned how to climb big cliffs, we gradually developed a strategy by which we could live our lives. More than that: we were in the process of escaping the confines of the valley and our home, into which the lottery of birth had thrown us. The style of our break-out was pre-programmed.

Günther Messner in the Brenta, Dolomites.

It is really not surprising that the heroic saga of Nanga Parbat gave wings to our pre-pubescent imaginations. While my fellow pupils were summoning the courage to make their first tentative approaches to girls, I was dreaming of Himalayan peaks. And I secretly hoped that one day I would go to Nanga Parbat. This dream became more and more intense and, more than a decade later, it became a reality.

Climbing had come to occupy a central role in my life. Everything else – job, girls, career – was pushed into the background. Now, the challenges I aspired to were the mountain summits, faces and ridges. These remote, high objectives were something tangible, the dangers they posed were concrete. There was an element of seriousness about them; every trip demanded total commitment. In those days, my life was all about commitment, discipline and the desire to break away from everything I had known before.

Climbing gave Günther and me an intensive feeling of companionship. It was not just that we were now part of that elite circle of extreme mountaineers; as brothers, we formed a very special partnership, planning and climbing everything together.

Back then, the alpine climbing scene was dominated by competition between the various partnerships, and by their willingness to take risks. Like the others, we were busy planning new routes, taking crazy ideas and hoping to make them work. It was certainly not just a case of bagging as many summits as possible; it was more a question of how we got there, since recognition amongst the little clique of extreme climbers was only given to those who were doing the hardest and most dangerous routes. Our style was characterized by a minimalist use of gear and the bold nature of our routes. For the young generation of climbers, the Rupal Face of Nanga Parbat became the epitome of this style of approach; it was a challenge that all of us found hard to imagine, but the climb that we all aspired to.

Meanwhile, Herrligkoffer was making more trips to Nanga Parbat. It was almost as if he still needed to work out how best to fulfil Merkl's legacy. Somehow Herrligkoffer had to finish what Merkl had started. Merely thinking about it was not going to get the job done, for in the fantasy world that he inhabited, 'German values' had to be 'victorious' in the end. The first ascent had been ten years previously.

Herrligkoffer: 'We naturally wished to see German climbers on the summit of the "German mountain of destiny".'

Again and again, and with new teams each time, this self-styled 'boss' set out to reconnoitre his mountain: from the west, from the south-west and finally from the south. Herrligkoffer led no fewer than four expeditions to the foot of the Rupal Face; it was as if his aim was to determine just what German mountaineers might be capable of achieving on the South Face. In 1968 a strong team failed just below the crux section of the Face, the so-called Merkl Icefield.

A few months later that same summer, my brother and I were on the hardest first ascent of our lives: the Central Pillar of the Heiligkreuzkofel. In a bivouac in a tiny cave in the middle of an overhanging rock face high above the Val Gardena in the Dolomites, and below the hardest part of our route, the headwall, Günther and I drank meltwater and waited for morning to come. Climbing was like therapy for us. Although Günther was battling with different traumas than I, we were both confident about what our lives would bring. Günther was unhappy with his career; I was obsessed by the idea of climbing higher, harder and further. We both wanted just one thing: to get away, far away – and soon.

The following morning we set off and climbed three short pitches to where the rock on the buttress turned yellow. This meant that the wall above us was overhanging and completely featureless. The only possibility of free climbing this section lay off to the right, so we traversed across as far as we could and had a look around. Placing a ring peg in a crack in the rock, I lowered off and pendulumed across to join a ramp line leading up to the right to a small platform on the vertical edge of the Pillar. So far, so good. The structure of the cliff – cracks, ledges and holds – had so far determined the line of the route we had followed. But what now? Which way to go? First of all, Günther had to second the pitch.

I had soon run out of ideas; the climbing was just too hard. I managed another couple of metres free; it was exceptionally difficuly, but it went. Then there was this tiny little pocket, about two or three centimetres deep. I hammered a short knife blade in and it held. Onwards. This was free climbing of an exceptionally severe nature. Finally I found a couple of larger holds. I stuck the peg hammer in my back pocket. With my fingers crammed into a narrow crack running up the back of a shallow groove, a series of bold free moves got me a little higher and after a few airy minutes I reached a narrow ledge, just wide enough to stand on.

The way ahead was unclear; a smooth slab with no cracks and hardly any holds blocked further progress but 4m higher I could see a crack. That was what I had to aim for. With nothing but fresh air and overhanging rock below me, I stood on the foothold ledge and tried to work it out. I couldn't go straight up, but perhaps it would go further to the right. The rock was too smooth out there, the holds too small. I was stuck.

Nevertheless, I refused to admit defeat; instead, I tried again and again to go straight up from my little perch. After thirty minutes of this, I had still failed to make a single move. Right, I would have to go down then! But even that was impossible. Without pegs I could not abseil, I could not reverse the moves to the knife blade and I wasn't brave enough to jump off.

Standing on the narrow foothold was starting to get strenuous and I wondered how on earth I was going to stand on the tiny edges a few metres higher – if I ever got that far. I was tired now; it was evening. But I could not go down. The only escape was up. I wondered whether to go for it, to take the risk. Again and again, I tried to make the move from the ledge; again and again I stepped back down to the same foothold. Thinking that I might have another go at reversing the moves below I had another quick look down. Soon, however, the capacity for logical thought returned. No, I couldn't reverse it. No chance. We were stuck: prisoners on an overhanging rock face. There was no way out.

I dried my fingertips one more time to get a better grip on the holds. *Back then we did not use chalk.*

'Right! This time! Four metres, that's all,' I muttered to myself and alerted my brother at the same time.

There was a tiny crimp at full stretch; just a few millimetres wide; just big enough for my fingernails. I went for it and got it. I was committed now but I could pull on the hold. I brought my right foot up and balanced up carefully onto it until I could reach up and curl the fingertips of my left hand around a sloping edge and pull through the move. Just a few more metres and I was standing on a roomy belay ledge, where I immediately banged a fat channel peg into a fist-wide crack, clipped in and proceeded to bring Günther up.

To save time Günther seconded the pitch on a tight rope. As we topped out, proud of ourselves and in high spirits, we both knew we had done something out of the ordinary.

What's more, we were still alive! In those days we were climbing on our own isolated little island. We climbed according to our own rules and were so infatuated with it all that we found any doubts that outsiders might have laughable. We were like sworn conspirators, sharing our own secret world. This feeling formed a bond far stronger than the bond of brothership. With every crux that we climbed, with every life-threatening situation that we returned from, our confidence grew. Whatever the future held, for us there was no longer anything impossible in the Alps.

It was in 1969 that the invitation to join an expedition to Nanga Parbat came crashing into this Wagnerian mood of self belief. It came unexpectedly; the chance to climb the Rupal Face, the biggest rock and ice face in the world. But the invitation was for me only and, furthermore, other climbers had advised me against going to the Himalaya with Herrligkoffer. In our little world, confusion reigned.

It seemed that in 1970 Karl Maria Herrligkoffer intended to mount one last attempt to reach the summit of Nanga Parbat by its most difficult face, the Rupal Flank, despite his lack of professionalism either as a climber or as an organizer and the fact that he was now fifty-four years old. The South Face of the mountain was again to be his objective, then; and German mountaineers were again to accompany him. Herrligkoffer said, 'I always was a nationalistic kind of man.' I knew that it was only because I was a German-speaking South Tyrolean climber that I was getting this invitation to join a Herrligkoffer expedition.

The invitation to go on the Rupal Face expedition surprised me at just that time of my life when I ought to have been starting out in middle-class life or, rather, it caught me as I was considering prolonging my youthful years as a 'conscientious objector against middle-class life' for a further decade or so. Assuming that I survived the trip I could still become a professional climber or a mountain guide, I reasoned – and with that, I accepted.

Günther felt rejected, however. He was hurt, but did not voice his disappointment directly. For a while, we each went our separate ways.

Günther and I belonged together. What we shared was like our own little fortress, in which we felt safe. On the mountain, where we had always repulsed any attack from outside, we were a team. After all, had we not developed our own strategies to escape the claustrophobic confines of South Tyrol, to seize our freedom, to allow us to determine our own future?

As brothers we were more, far more, than just a climbing partnership. We had our own lifestyle, our own secrets: routes that we planned to climb, dreams that we shared, and a mutual zest for life.

Chapter VII

Nanga Parbat at Any Price

Nanga Parbat from the east with the Rupal Face on the left.

With Nanga Parbat as the objective, our secret kingdom that we had founded on our first independent climbs together received a new dimension. Although we knew that the mountain had been climbed, the myth lived on, particularly on the Rupal Face. This myth had an astonishing power, and we were quite prepared to leave all the logistics to the expedition leadership. We would have gone with the devil himself to Nanga Parbat.

Günther Messner

Dr Herrligkoffer, the 'leader'.

For many years it has seemed to me that leading an
expedition up the Rupal Face to emerge victorious on
the summit of Nanga Parbat is a goal worth striving for.
Karl Maria Herrligkoffer

The Rupal Face! Imagine this: the East Face of Monte
Rosa with the Eigerwand above and the Matterhorn
perched on top. In fact, the Rupal Face is impossible
for anyone to imagine unless they have actually seen it.
From the earliest days, this huge flank has impressed all
those who have passed beneath it. Now it is our turn.
We are consumed by the thought of climbing it, caught
up in a mixture of hope and fear. This face is the
greatest mountaineering challenge of my life!
Reinhold Messner

We see the Rupal Flank dropping steeply from the
summit, the objective of our desires – huge, terrifying, and
seemingly impenetrable. Would we conquer it this time?
Karl Maria Herrligkoffer

Departure for Nanga Parbat

Once my participation in the 'Sigi Löw Memorial Expedition' to Nanga Parbat was confirmed, a lively exchange of letters began between me and Dr Karl Maria Herrligkoffer, the leader of the expedition. It was all about equipment, members who dropped out, appointments and deadlines. In a letter dated 14.12.1969, Dr Herrligkoffer informed me that my friend Sepp Mayerl had decided to pull out and join a different expedition. The postscript said 'Can you think of a substitute?' I immediately thought of Günther, as I knew of no better partner. Günther was so enthusiastic that at first he did not dare to believe he might actually get invited.

Two weeks later I put a telegram under the Christmas tree for him. It read: 'AGREEABLE WITH GÜNTHER. KARL.'

Over the winter, we had time to read up on Nanga Parbat. Günther was working as a bank clerk in Bruneck; I was supply teaching in a middle school. We had to earn the money to pay our share of the expedition's costs. In our minds, we were already on our way, somewhere in deepest Asia, in the Himalaya.

We had spoken about the mountain again and again, thought about it, dreamed about it. When the first reports appeared in the newspapers my pupils pinned a drawing to the wall. The headline said 'Messner boys to go to Nanga Parbat.'

During the winter we embarked upon a special training regime: plenty of running, breathing exercises, abandoning upper body-strength workouts in favour of specific muscle-strengthening exercises for the legs. My pupils took the greatest pleasure in competing against me. We invented an exercise we called the 'non-stop relay', a brand new athletics' discipline.

For the whole of the PE lesson, the entire class would race, one after another, against the teacher, who had to keep going without a break. I chose the course myself. We took it in turns to win.

I also had to try to explain to them how high Nanga Parbat was. It was hard to do with numbers alone, so I tried it with mountains:

'Camp 1 will be at the height of Mont Blanc and the plan is to have five camps. The summits of the highest of our South Tyrol mountains would reach to just above Base Camp. If you piled two Ortlers one on top of the other and then stuck the Cima Ovest on top, the whole thing would probably reach up to the South Shoulder. From there to the summit it is not even another hundred metres of vertical height but that last steep rise is tougher than doing a run over the mountains from Bozen to Jenesien because the air is so thin up there. It is the same on all of the high mountains, and Nanga Parbat is a very high mountain.'

The school kids had read somewhere that there would be a doctor on the expedition, a doctor who was also going to lead the expedition. They now wanted to know what there was for a doctor to do. I told them that he was there to administer first aid, to splint or plaster broken legs and to treat frostbite, to explain the effect of the stimulants and look after the sick and injured. A doctor was very important on an expedition, I told them, and he should also be able to get as high as possible on the mountain.

The grown-ups had plenty of questions, too. We found ourselves having to explain to them over and over again how high the mountain was and how steep the face, what the enterprise was going to cost and for which day the 'summit assault' was planned. I hope that I did not get my facts and figures mixed up in the confusion of so many questions: 8125m high, 60 degree slope, 130,000DM, and we should be on the summit around the time of summer solstice, between the 20th and 22nd of June. I had to have all the answers off pat, and trot them out in every conceivable combination.

I was doing just that in reply to an old acquaintance I had happened to bump into just before we set off. 'I would never have the time just to wander around for months on end like that,' he said, adding that he had to go into hospital. The diagnosis was hardening of the arteries. Too little exercise, the doctors said. We will be away for about the same time, I thought; he in some clinic or other, I will be on Nanga Parbat. But Nanga Parbat was not just some mountain or other, and the Rupal Flank was not just any old mountain face.

Günther set off with eleven of the team members at the beginning of April. A convoy of trucks loaded with 9 tons of equipment was taking the overland route to Asia. In his letters, Günther wrote about each stage of that exciting journey: Teheran, the filthy city of Kabul, the Khyber Pass.

On 16th April his first letter arrived:

Ankara, 12.4.1970, 9 o'clock (local time)
To all at home,
We reached the capital city of Turkey about an hour ago. It is an endless sea of lights, a city of millions. Our trucks are going straight to customs and if we are lucky they will be ready tomorrow and we'll be able to carry on early on Tuesday. So finally we get the chance to spend a little time in a city. By the way, our trucks are running splendidly; we were easily able to make up the five and a half hours we spent waiting at the Bulgarian–Turkish border. We managed about 560km today (we spent the night 100km from Istanbul in quite a run-down little hotel). In Istanbul we picked up a qualified mechanic whose job it was to check our trucks for any damage on the leg to Ankara (one or two little things had broken, as it turned out). He piloted us through the metropolis of Istanbul (after a brief stop at the port) and at half past eight we took the ferry across to 'Asia'. From Yugoslavia through Bulgaria to the west coast of Turkey the landscape hardly changed at all. You see

donkeys instead of horses, sheep and goats instead of pigs and the people wear different clothes. The fruit trees are in full bloom in the big orchards near the coast. We were only 200km from Ankara when I clearly noticed the change to the karst and desert landscape of the Middle East. Our hotel here in Ankara is on a main road and the noise is worse than an Italian pub! The cars drive by honking their horns constantly. Almost all of the shops are still open and the road is still (!) being asphalted. Hopefully we will find another hotel for tomorrow night.

Love,
Günther

Back home, people were talking more and more about Nanga Parbat. For some, it was the 'Mountain of Destiny of the Germans', for others it was my particular 'eccentricity'. Some thought it impossible. For Karl Maria Herrligkoffer it was his mountain. For us, the ones who wanted to climb it, it was the most beautiful mountain in the world.

At the end of April I flew from Munich to Rawalpindi with the expedition leader Herrligkoffer and a small rearguard team. At Munich Airport I was asked if we wanted to go to the summit of Nanga Parbat. I presume the woman who posed the question meant my brother Günther and me. I shrugged my shoulders, unable to answer such a stupid question. My school kids had never asked me questions like that; they took it for granted that Günther and I wanted to get to the top, why else would we be going to the Himalaya?

On 26th April I met up with Günther again in the Pakistani city of Rawalpindi. Our expedition was to lose several valuable days there, waiting to fly out to Gilgit, so we strolled around the bazaars, excited and full of expectations. All the expedition members addressed each other by their first names and I now got to know a few of them a little better.

Many of my first impressions were later to be confirmed:

KARL (HERRLIGKOFFER), the grey-haired expedition leader; taciturn and reserved.

FELIX (KUEN), an army mountain guide from North Tyrol; behaves like a predestined 'summit victor', although uncertain of himself; grimly determined.

PETER (SCHOLZ) from Munich. A quiet man, simple and straightforward. Knows the Rupal Face from the 1968 attempt; enjoys the respect of all.

WERNER (HAIM), like Kuen, an army guide, but big-hearted and very helpful. The happy Tyrolean!

MAX (BARON VON KIENLIN) is here as a guest. Born in 1934, he wanted to go on an expedition and see the site of the Merkl tragedy for himself; just along for the ride.

GERHARD (BAUR) is as good a climber as he is a film maker; young, enthusiastic and high-spirited. Here to make a film of the expedition.

HANS (SALER), a Munich man; a real adventurer. Finds it impossible to come to terms with routine middle-class life.

GINE (GÜNTHER KROH), from Swabia, an excellent rock climber with a mischievous look in his eye; knows how to laugh.

HERMANN (KÜHN), scientist and mountaineer – and passionate about both. A great man.

JÜRGEN (WINKLER), the famous photographer and mountaineer; a well balanced personality. His job is to document the trip.

PETER (VOGLER) is still very young and subordinate. Unfortunately he is often sick.

GERHARD (MÄNDL) from Munich, an all-round mountaineer. Tough, eager for action; also willing to subordinate himself to the leadership.

ELMAR (RAAB) is a born helper. A man of many talents; later to organize the supply chain to the top camps.

WOLFI (BITTERLING) is the son of the Bitterling who took part in the 1953 expedition; like his father, not an experienced top climber. But his cooking is excellent.

Felix Kuen   Peter Scholz   Alice von Hobe
                                     (Alex)

Michl Anderl   Gerhard Mändl   Günther Messner

Wolfi Bitterling   Gerhard Baur   Werner Haim

110

Elmar Raab   *Hans Saler*   *Max von Kienlin*

Günther Kroh   *Dr Hermann Kühn*   *Peter Vogler*

The 1970 team. With the exception of Herrligkoffer's assistant Alice von Hobe, Wolfi Bitterling and guest Max von Kienlin they were all experienced mountaineers, the elite of German-speaking mountaineering in the 1970s.

Jürgen Winkler

111

ALICE (VON HOBE), Herrligkoffer's aide at Base Camp; accompanies him whenever he goes out on his excursions.

MICHL (ANDERL), a member of the old school, tough and experienced. Unfortunately, like Herrligkoffer, he lacks leadership skills.

CAPTAIN (SAQI) is our liaison officer; a big, well-built young man who takes his job seriously.

And finally, 15 HUNZA porters, known as the 'TIGERS', were to be engaged, without whom the expedition would have failed.

We had got used to our active leisure time while waiting in Rawalpindi, often swimming in the pool at the Hotel Intercontinental, and were well practised in the art of haggling over our purchases by the time we were finally ready to go. We flew in a Hercules to Gilgit, then on to Nanga Parbat.

In Gilgit we wrote postcards:

7th May 1970

To all at home,
Today we finally managed to get a flight to Gilgit. The baggage, however, is still back in Rawalpindi, where we have just had ten days' 'on holiday'. I enjoyed it (despite being annoyed about our pathetic leadership), I am browner than I've ever been in my life before and I had plenty of opportunities to learn about life in the Orient. There's lots to tell.
Greetings,
Reinhold

As well as the official expedition journal, Günther also kept his own private diary. It begins with our departure from Gilgit.

Tuesday, 12 May 1970
Departure from Gilgit at 5a.m. Five Jeeps, loaded with personal gear. Exciting drive up the Gilgit River. A magnificent river bed; very exposed. After Bunji we follow the Indus

112

heading for the Astor Bridge. After crossing the Indus, Nanga stood there before us. Views of the Rakhiot side with the Fairy Meadow, Rakhiot Peak, the Moor's Head, Silver Saddle, Silver Plateau, *Silberzacken* and the Summit, just like the photos. It doesn't look like 8000m. Our mountain (we intend to climb it from the South side) looks different. The greatest mountaineering challenge of our time waits there for us.

Beyond Ramghat we catch up with the tractors carrying the bulk of the expedition's equipment. Difficult drive along a river bed; no road. A tractor tips over sideways. One of the porters sustains a minor injury to his leg. On we go, across incredible terrain to just before the Astor Bridge. Here, the baggage is loaded onto Jeeps. Reinhold and I walk on ahead and after about 2km we meet the first of the porters ferrying the loads up to Astor.

It is late by the time most of the loads have been distributed. We divide our time between helping out and lying in the sun on a big rock next to the foaming Astor River. In the late afternoon, most of the expedition leaves the spot where the loads were divided up. Michael Anderl, Elmar Raab, Peter Scholz and I stay behind to sort out the rest of the loads tomorrow. Cold bath in the Astor River. Fresh-air bivi next to the road; fabulous starry sky and lots of shooting stars; porters lying with their donkeys right next to us.

Günther sat up late into the night, thinking about the men who had been on Nanga Parbat before us: Mummery, Merkl, Buhl. The next day he wrote in his diary:

Wednesday, 13 May 1970
Michl wakes me in the morning and sends me off to the others to search for some missing petrol canisters. Carrying a little rucksack I leave the equipment depot and head for Astor. It is five o'clock in the morning. At half eight I bump into the team in Hardschir, about 10 miles from Astor. A long stretch of the Astor road is damaged and impassable,

even for the Jeeps. I carry on walking and at 12 o'clock I am in Astor (2600m). Reinhold has been here since morning.

Herrligkoffer: 'Captain Saqi is furious that Herr von Kienlin and Reinhold Messner have again disregarded his orders and the 'Government Rules' and the expedition has not marched as a group.'

Max and I had made friends and we often went along together on the walk-in. We were not keen on marching through these mountain valleys in a big crowd.

Günther Messner: 'Found lodgings at the school in Astor. The rest of the team arrives during the course of the afternoon. Most of the loads do, too.

Stroll through Astor; refreshing bath in the river; filming, taking photographs. Apricots and nuts still growing up here. Invitation from the Doctor of the Valley.'

From Günther's diary:

Thursday 14 May 1970

We set off at seven o'clock for a daring Jeep ride to Rampur (approx. 24km). Reinhold leaves us on foot at six and gets to the rest house in Rampur at almost the same time as us. Brief rest and a snack.

Then it's on foot to Tarshing (2900m). Reinhold and I go on ahead, get lost and lose time; the rest of the team is now ahead of us. Reinhold catches them up. I meet up with Max, who is also doing the majority of the approach march on foot, and together with Peter Vogler we arrive at Tarshing in the afternoon in pouring rain. We put up at the school and dry our clothes out in front of an open fire. We sit in the smoke-filled room with our tea, eggs, rice and chapatti. Sepp, an experienced high-altitude porter with eleven expeditions to his name, looks after us like a mother. No one else seems bothered about us. Each of us has to 'muddle along' as best he can.

114

Nanga Parbat and the Rupal Valley from Astor.

The loads again arrive in dribs and drabs; they will be redistributed tomorrow.

Friday, 15 May 1970

The day dawns bright and cloudless. For the first time I see Nanga and Chongra Peak from the south: the impression is overwhelming. Huge hanging glaciers, terrifying precipices, furrowed by avalanches. Right over to the left is the summit of Nanga! There are questions here that no one can answer; the answers lie in the future.

115

Porters and their loads at Base Camp.

We set off for Rupal as a group. Reinhold and I are a bit faster and go on ahead. Leaving the mountain village of Rupal behind us, we encounter farmers using age-old methods of clearing the ground to gain new land for planting. Nanga is unfortunately now stuck in the clouds; they only part now and then, but the terrifically high and steep rock and ice flanks that we can see give a tantalizing foretaste of what lies hidden: the highest mountain face in the world.

We cross the outflow of a huge glacier and Tap Alpe comes into view, where Base Camp will be situated. We search around and try to find a good location for a camp site. Nanga is still shrouded in cloud. We carry on to the 'Rupal Lake'. Max arrives, followed later by Karl. It is not long before a little village of tents is pitched beneath the Rupal Flank.

116

Base Camp.

Base Camp, Saturday 16 May 1970
First day at Base Camp.
Reinhold, Gert Mändl, Hans Saler, two porters and I set off
from Base Camp at half three in the morning to fix the gully
to Camp 1. We fix 200m of rope to the upper end of the
gully. Reinhold, Sepp (the best Hunza porter) and I push on
to the 1968 Camp 1. We sort out a place there for our Camp
1. Eight o'clock. Hans Saler and Gert Mändl come up. On
the way back down we fix the gully from top to bottom. We
are back at the main camp by eleven o'clock. The afternoon
is spent sorting gear out and packing our personal kit for
Camp 1.

That evening Herrligkoffer tore us off a strip. He said that

117

Günther and I should follow his orders and not climb as a team any longer, but I insisted on having Günther as my partner.

From Günther's diary:

Camp 1 (4700m), Sunday, 17 May 1970
At two o'clock in the morning, Werner Haim, Peter Scholz, Reinhold and I set off to establish Camp 1. We each carry our personal kit (approx. 25kg). Three porters follow later with tents and food. We finally decide to opt for the new camp-site rather than the one used by the 1968 expedition. We all agree that the camp is safe. We take turns with the snow shovels, working excitedly and with great enthusiasm. It takes hours until a space big enough to take four tents (two for four sahibs, two for six porters) and the kitchen has been dug out. We sort out the loads for Camp 2. During the course of the morning, Saler, Mändl and a few porters come up to Camp 1. The sun only hits our tents at eleven o'clock but then it gets unbearably hot. There is no longer any talk of work. I can't even sleep. My body feels tired and listless and the cold I have had since Gilgit prevents me from breathing properly. We are now at about the same height as Mont Blanc but I don't notice the lack of oxygen. The provisional times for radio calls with Base Camp are twelve o'clock and six in the evening. We go to bed early. Glorious weather, great views.

Camp 1 (4700m), Whit Monday, 18 May 1970
Today is my birthday. I am 24 years old. I get to celebrate it at Camp 1 on the Rupal Flank. I am lying in the tent. During the day the heat is murderous and the meltwater runs off the overhanging walls onto our tents. We had set off at midnight to fix the Wieland Rocks; Peter Scholz, Werner Haim, Reinhold and I. We took a wire cable, carabiners, pitons and 400m of normal rope. Sepp came along as the only porter. We fixed the ropes from the top down whilst descending. We've been back at Camp 1 since sunrise. Reinhold and Peter Scholz are not feeling too well. They haven't eaten anything warm

for a long time. Max has now arrived (during the night, he and Hans Saler missed the path to Camp 1 and had to make some diversions). Our Leader arrives later. Felix, Michael and Hans are also here and the first big column of porters. Max stays with us and spoils us rotten.

That same lunchtime, I wrote in my diary:
                    Camp 1 (4700m), Monday, 18 May
Midday. We are lying in the tent. The heat is murderous. The water that drips from the overhangs runs like quicksilver over the tent flysheet. Like lizards crawling across the sky.

As long as the sun is not burning mercilessly down on the camp we extend Camp 1, pitch another porters' tent, sort out provisions and equipment, erect a tarp over the tents and organize the kitchen.

The sun goes down at 5 o'clock at Camp 1. We are out of the heat at last. We now organize the loads for the carry to Camp 2 tomorrow.

While one group is busy extending Camp 1 further, Günther, Werner and I are to go up and occupy Camp 2. The team at Camp 1 provisionally takes on the job of supplying Camp 2, together with three high altitude porters. We are learning how a Himalayan expedition functions: the load carries, the route finding and the establishment of a chain of high camps. Günther and I are a team within a team.

This is Günther's diary entry for the next day:
                    Camp 2, Tuesday, 19 May 1970
We have established Camp 2 beneath a 30m-high vertical ice wall. To begin with there is just one tent, for Werner, Reinhold and me.

We reached the new campsite with the porters in glorious sunshine between six and seven in the morning. Marvellous all-round views. Mountains nearby and far away on the horizon. To the east, Broad Peak (H. Buhl), K2 (Lacedelli)

At Camp 2.

and many others whose names I do not know. To the west, quite close, unclimbed five- and six-thousanders dominating the inner Rupal cirque. Probably all still unclimbed.

Camp 2, like Camp 1, is safe from avalanches. The masses of snow thundering down from above the seracs split and funnel down to the right and left of the camp.

Here at Camp 2 the sun goes down at two o'clock, which means we can sleep in the afternoons without worrying about frying in the cosmic radiation. One of the porters has stopped at the beginning of the Wieland Glacier and gone back down. It's a shame.

The Wieland Rocks and the Glacier now have fixed ropes in place. Reinhold has recovered since yesterday and is in excellent form. Peter Scholz has gone back down to Base Camp. Unfortunately we don't have a stove so we have to satisfy our hunger with tinned food.

From my diary:

Camp 2, Wednesday, 20 May 1970

Outside, the wind is blowing hard. The snow sloughs off the roof of the tent at regular intervals. We picture to ourselves the next few days in a snow storm. We can still smile about this, our first, spell of bad weather. Gallows humour?

There are still three of us here at Camp 2: Werner, Günther and I. Early this morning Günther and I fetched a load of rope and pegs from the lower end of the Wieland Glacier. Four porters, along with Gert, Hans and Gerhard had got that far and dropped their loads before descending again immediately.

It started snowing hard towards midday. The wind is now tugging at the tent. Werner says there is 15cm of new snow outside already. I am going to read (a collection of stories by Russian authors), brew tea and get plenty of sleep.

If it is still snowing tomorrow we are going to run short of food.

Camp 2, Thursday, 21 May 1970

Today we've even got a cook! Gert cooks a meal for us. It does us good. We will soon have been on the mountain for a week.

We were woken at four this morning by the voices of Gerhard and Gert. Soon afterwards we set off to fix the ice wall below Camp 3. The bergschrund was difficult, the snow brittle. I ran out and fixed all the ropes up to the rocks while Gerhard filmed.

Four porters arrived in the meantime. By the time Günther, Werner and I get back, Peter has also arrived from Base Camp, so now there are six of us.

It is one o'clock. The sun has just disappeared behind a huge bulge of ice. It is getting pleasant in the tents now. I sleep, dream and my thoughts turn to things that you don't get up here. Tomorrow morning we want to descend to Base Camp and have a 'washday'.

Base Camp (3600m), Friday 22 May 1970

Down from Camp 2 to Base Camp in just 50 minutes but my muscles are aching so badly now that I'm regretting the headlong chase. Every one is still asleep at Base Camp when I arrive. Tea and chapattis with the porters.

Spent the morning, the afternoon, the whole day long washing stuff – just relaxing and washing.

The next day Günther wrote a letter to our mother, with whom we both had a particularly intimate relationship. After all, it was she who was the calming influence in our big family. If anyone understood us, it was she, and in spite of feeling anxious about what we were doing she shared our enthusiasm.

Base Camp, 23.5.1970

Dear Mama,

Yesterday morning Reinhold and I came back down from Camp 2 for a rest day.

We finally established Base Camp here on the Tap Alpe at 3560m on 15 May, after a series of seemingly insurmountable difficulties. The Rupal Face, the South Face of Nanga Parbat, is bigger and more impressive than I imagined. It is an incredible 4500m of vertical height from Base Camp to the summit and no mountain face in the Western Alps can compare with the steepness and the wild aspect. The North Face of the Ortler, for example, is a joke by comparison. Then there is the altitude. Base Camp (3560m), Camp 1 (4700m) – almost as high as Mont Blanc! – Camp 2 (5500m). So far, Reinhold, Werner Haim and I have fixed ropes between Base Camp and Camp 3 (approx. 6000m) and have established Camps 1 and 2 with the help of some outstanding Hunza high-altitude porters. We have also acclimatized, more or less. Unfortunately I have still got a bit of a cold, which makes breathing at altitude more difficult. I am hoping it will clear up here at Base Camp. It's a marvellous feeling to have done almost everything on our own so far, without having to listen to our leader's complaints. Tomorrow or the day after we will be setting off for Camp 2 again (almost 2000m height gain) and then establishing Camp 3 (6000m). So far the weather has been glorious and during the day it is so hot that work on the face is impossible. You can't even sleep, just wait for the shade to cool things off. At night it is minus 10–20°C. That is the only time any work gets done. We are in good shape and the high-altitude porters are silently impressed with us. They work more or less according to our suggestions.

(I'll have to be quick – the mail runner has just arrived and is about to set off back down!)
Greetings from the Himalaya
Günther and Reinhold

Meanwhile, I was writing to my little brother Hubert:

We are filthy and sunburned but in the best of moods. We have now pitched two camps and fixed ropes all the way to Camp 3. We've already been to 6000m! For the time being there is another lead team up there. Tomorrow, at one o'clock in the morning, we will go back up to occupy Camp 2 and will establish Camp 3 from there. That is when the real difficulties begin. We've got to do it in the next three weeks, otherwise that's it. Sitting here it is hard to imagine that the Rupal Face is 4500m high. The Face is every bit as steep as the steepest walls in the Western Alps and sections of it are bloody difficult.

123

I guess school will be finished for you soon and it will be summer in Europe.

It was three days later before we could get back on the face. Felix and Peter were already up there. They managed to dig out and repair the cable winch that the 1968 team had used to haul loads between Camp 2 and Camp 3.

From my diary:

Camp 2, Tuesday, 26 May 1970
Got here from Base Camp in 3½ hours – almost 2000m of height gain. I had to break trail on the upper part of the Wieland Glacier as the porters were still on their way up. Günther came up a little later. He is in great form.

Winch Camp (5900m), Thursday, 28 May 1970
The load winch between Camp 2 and Camp 3 is working today for the first time. I climb up alongside the loads. They keep getting stuck. Freeing the plastic barrels, climbing up, then down again to free another stuck load is a real grind. At around midday we are up: two loads and I. I sort out my campsite. The route of the load-hauling cable has to be repositioned further over to the left. We hope the barrels will slide better over there.

Winch Camp, Friday, 29 May 1970
Three tons of gear winched up – real drudgery.
   Günther follows us up to the Winch Camp. In the afternoon we recce the route to Camp 3. Had a bit of luck this time when searching for the campsite. I had positioned Camp 1 because it was so glaringly obvious. There was no better site. I had found the site for Camp 2 after hours of searching. It had a lot going for it and I was well pleased with my find. I hadfound Camp 3 today by pure chance. I had fixed ropes up to the site of the old Camp 3 and was tired. I was not happy with the site and was wandering about a bit

Günther Messner prepares a meal at the Ice Dome (Camp 3).

when, by coincidence, I broke through into a crevasse. I hacked away to make the hole bigger and soon discovered the ideal site for the camp: an ice cave, 6m deep and a good 4m wide, with a vaulted roof. We call it the 'Ice Dome'!

The next day I scribbled another quick entry in my diary:

Ice Dome (6000m), 30 May 1970
Still no tents here. Felix and I dig out the site. A kitchen has been installed. I am getting to like this place more and more. The Ice Dome is safe and roomy.

We hauled up another 3 tons this morning. Mind-numbing work. Tomorrow we hope finally to move into the Ice

Dome (Camp 3). Just one more night in the tiny, wet tents at Winch Camp. The Hunzas are going to take over the work of ferrying loads. The winch is working perfectly now. During the morning, the mist came down. Now, in the evening, it is clear again. The valleys are in shadow. Peter plays his mouth organ. For a few hours, I forget that we are on the Rupal Flank.

Herrligkoffer: 'At the end of May, the third camp was extended to provide an acclimatization camp. This year, shelter for the tents was provided by an ice cave located at the site we already knew about from our previous visit. The Messner brothers fixed 200m of line to safeguard the route through the lower Welzenbach Icefield.'

Ice Dome, 1 June 1970

It is late now. I am writing my last notes by candlelight. The expedition is now making good progress.

Peter and Felix have fixed the route as far as the first cliffs on the Welzenbach Icefield. Günther and I then went up to join them and took over, intending to run out more rope up the Icefield and the Welzenbach Couloir. 100m below the planned site for Camp 4 it got too late. We abseiled off: 700m of terrain similar to the Ortler and the North Face of the Matterhorn. Very exposed!

Ice Dome, 2 June 1970

Rest day. Happy just being here, sitting, waiting, breathing. We actually wanted to go up and look for a site for Camp 4 but then decided we were too tired and stayed in the tent. This mountaineering leaves precious little time for distractions, pleasures and entertainment. Climbing at this altitude and in this area is a tough business that calls for a real effort of will.

You think only about the cold, the thin air, life within the cramped confines of the tent. Then there are the dangers, the damp, and frequently tiredness to contend with.

Günther Messner during the retreat.

And tomorrow we will be setting off anyway. No one is forcing us to do it, but we must go higher.

Ice Dome, 3 June 1970
Felix, Peter, Günther and I set off for Camp 4 at five o'clock this morning. The weather was good and we soon put the first 400m behind us. Then the ice blanked out and it started snowing; little snow slides kept coming down. Only the last 100m to the ice bulge still had to be fixed.

It was afternoon before we reached the place where the 1968 Camp 4 had stood. There it really began to blow hard. We could hardly make ourselves understood, as the snowstorm increased in strength minute by minute. One of us dug a hole in the snow, Peter threw his bivi bag in and we all buried our loads before descending immediately,

127

keeping to the fixed ropes – more than 800m in all. Everyone had a real fight with the icy ropes. Even our crampons sometimes slipped on the hard ice. In spite of all this we carried on down and at 5 p.m. we were all safely back at Camp 3. The hardest day on Nanga so far. Dangerous, too.

But how good it was to be able to determine the logistics ourselves, at least.

Herrligkoffer: 'In the first few days of June another 400m were fixed in the Welzenbach Couloir. This terrain is comparable with the North Face of the Matterhorn. On 3 June the route to the fourth high camp was finally equipped with fixed ropes.' If the expedition leader only knew what his comments really meant. But then again, he is not a climber.

My diary later helped jog my memory of events:
Ice Dome, 4 June 1970
It has been snowing all night. The wind is blowing snow into our cave – a metre deep. Outside, the new snow is higher than our tents. Our tent is bent and creased. The side walls are wet and sagging and pressing against our sleeping bags. Everything is getting wet. I have crammed my down jacket between the wall of the tent and my down sleeping bag, but it doesn't help much. The situation is hopeless. If it doesn't stop we will have to get used to the idea of being snowed in. We have got food for a few days. We've also got a stove in the tent, luckily.

Felix spent hours looking for the shovel this morning. Now he has it. He and Günther take turns shovelling snow out of the cave. It's snowing faster than they can shovel it away but they want to keep the entrances free at least. We decide to do an hour's snow clearing each.

I talked to Gerhard about the film today; we discussed ideas, suggestions and plans. What a lot you can say with moving pictures. It is still snowing. The guys on snow duty are still busy outside, shovelling away.

Against the Wall

The higher up the mountain we climbed, the more spartan and cramped life became. To save weight, the tents were small and flat; the petrol stoves were awkward to use, and the provisions had to be stored in snow holes and crevices in the rocks. There was hardly any room to keep our few personal items dry. High-altitude mountaineering is not a pleasure; it is a total misery.

From my diary:

Ice Dome, 5 June 1970, 7 p.m.
Spent the whole day in the tent. Outside, more than a metre of new snow had fallen again. No need to panic, though. It is astonishing how quickly I shake off the bustle and the habits of my everyday life when I am in the mountains for a long period. Things that were important a month ago now leave me completely apathetic. So I lie quietly in my tent and let it snow. I am simply there – in an ice cave, at 6000m above sea level. The roof of the tent is full of ice crystals that glisten in the candlelight. Strange Nirvana.

Ice Dome, 6 June 1970
It is still snowing. At midday Peter and Felix go down to Base Camp. Günther and I decide to stay to keep the camp intact. We are hoping for better weather. Apart from shovelling snow, there's not much to do, so we read, chat, melt lots of snow and cook. Günther and I complement each other splendidly.

Ice Dome, 7 June 1970

It's snowing again. But it has got colder. Otherwise everything is the same: cooking, clearing snow. We make radio contact with Base Camp every three hours. We still have some food left. The petrol looks as if it will last, too.

Snowed in at Camp 3

Two tents in an ice cave. Icicles hanging from the roof. It is snowing. The wind whips powder snow into the gap behind the tents. More than a metre of new snow is lying in front of the tent on the left. Günther is about to go and clear it.

'Watch out that we don't get too much snow inside, or everything will be wet again tomorrow,' says a voice in the tent. A white cap emerges through the slit, followed by a head. The slim face is sunburnt and ravaged by the wind, the lips swollen and cracked. He slides his body out of the tent like a snake. Standing between the tent entrance and the wall of snow, he zips up the entrance again. Then he pulls the shovel out of the pile of snow and starts clearing the mass of snow away from the tent.

We had now been alone up there for four days. The camps below were all empty. Yet we still felt safe and well.

Günther is completely white, plastered in snow; he has cleared the space outside the tents of snow and now he chops ice from the wall of the cave and throws the pieces into a plastic bag. Then he goes to the other tent, takes a few tins from a blue bag lying in the entrance and opens up the tarps.

'Have you finished?' I ask.

'It's no use.'

130

'We'll go down tomorrow. There's no point staying up here.'

'Or anywhere else.'

'It will be warmer down there. We could at least get a proper wash.'

'Stop moaning; you sound like the others,' says Günther. He is holding a tin.

'Do you like chicken soup?' he asks as an afterthought. He throws the tin into the tent.

'Is it the last one?'

'Yes, last one.'

Günther knocks the snow off his clothing, puts the bag of ice inside the tent and throws another tin inside. Then he sits in the tent with just his boots poking outside. He takes them off, bangs them together and lifts them into the tent.

Günther is now back inside his sleeping bag, which he pulls up to his chest. It looks like he's trying to get the stove working. He crouches over it first, then picks it up, looks at it and carefully sets it down again. He tries unsuccessfully to light it. It doesn't work, so he gives up.

'Don't you want to try again?' I ask.

'I've already tried everything. Give me a drop of petrol in the little coffee jar, please,' he says and picks up the stove again.

'Did I tell you the weather is going to get better?' I throw this into the conversation.

'Who says?'

'Karl said it. I've just radioed down.'

I fill the empty coffee jar with petrol and hand it to Günther to warm the stove with.

'We were right to wait it out then. So why did some of them not want us to stay up here?'

'Because they wanted to go down.'

'You've got to be able to cope with a bit of snow if you want to climb an eight-thousander.'

The stove is now going. Günther puts a pan on top, places a few pieces of ice in it and lies down again.

'What did we do yesterday?'

131

The South-East Face of Nanga Parbat with the South-East Buttress in profile.

'Nothing special. Same as always: shovelled snow, fetched ice. You did the cooking.'

I take a rust-coloured notebook out of the side pocket in the tent: my diary. We have to write it up for Karl, so he will know later what happened up on the mountain.

'Now I remember. We wrote our diaries and letters yesterday afternoon as well.'

I read the last page in my diary:

Ice Dome – Camp 3, 8 June

30 minutes of sun this morning! New hope. Now it is

evening and the cold is more biting than ever. Bad radio reception – should be a sign of good weather.

But it's snowing.

This lousy weather has lasted six days now. Spindrift, cold and wet in the tent. Big avalanches come down regularly but they can't hit us. The wave of spindrift from one of the avalanches still buries the tent completely at about 7:30 in the evening. Masses of spindrift!

I flip over the page and start writing, mouthing the words as I go:

Ninth-of-June-Ice-Dome-Camp-3-The-bad-weather-still-continues-but-the-morning-sun-gets-our-hopes-up-a-little-Günther-has-shovelled-the-snow-away-I-went-down-to-the-Winch-Camp-to-fetch-some-provisions-Could-hardly-see-the -tents-Two-hours-spent-shovelling-snow-Waded-waist-deep-in-snow-on-the-way-back-Spindrift-in-the-afternoon.

Meanwhile, down at Base Camp, they were drafting a plan for the summit push. Without us. Günther and I were simply part of the inventory, to do with as they wished.

Herrligkoffer: 'It is the 8th of June. Today I presented my plan of attack for those present to debate as a group. We discussed it point by point, taking note of any little suggestions and alterations and after about an hour we had agreed on all the details. The summit push is scheduled to take place in the last two days of a ten-day load-ferrying and camp-occupancy system that will be organized like a pyramid. The push will be led by two teams, with Reinhold Messner and Peter Scholz out at the front, followed immediately by Felix Kuen and Gerd Mändl, accompanied by the cameraman Baur. Should any of the climbers have to drop out, Werner Haim will substitute for Felix Kuen and Hans Saler for Gerd Baur. After the two named teams have reached the summit, further participants may follow as long as there is no risk of bad weather and the teams coming down do not require the help of the others to descend.'

Initially we learned nothing of this plan up at Camp 3. We just sat half-way up the face and wrote letters.

Rupal Face – Camp 3: Ice Dome, 8.6.1970

To all at home,

The writing paper has run out. The pages in my diary are nearly finished, too.

Günther and I are lying next to each other in a three-man tent, writing. We have been snowed in here for five days now with no let up in the storm or the snowfall. On 3.6. we tried with Peter Scholz and Felix Kuen to establish Camp 4. We got to 6600m before a heavy snow storm forced us to retreat. Our companions then went back down to Base Camp. We want to stay up at Camp 3 until the weather improves; the tents would not be able to stand up to the pressure of the snow unoccupied. Every day a metre of new snow falls and there are storm-force winds. It gets down to 20°C below zero. We still have enough food for three days. All the camps below us are empty. We had pork for lunch today. It did us good in this cold. We still have one tin of cranberries left for our evening meal. We are drinking a lot of tea and coffee – the Phöbus stove is steaming away constantly inside the tent. Luckily we have got plenty of petrol at the camp.

Our tent is pitched in a cave. It's a good job, too, otherwise the avalanches would sweep it away or the storm would tear it to shreds. But the snow still blows in. Every morning we have to squirm out of the top of the entrance to shovel the tent free of snow. Every six hours we have radio contact with Base Camp – just! Well, at least that way they know down there that we're still alive.

This period of bad weather has been a serious setback to our attempts to push the route. Before it set in everything was going smoothly. In the space of just two weeks we managed 3000m of vertical height and 4000m of climbing and fixed ropes on almost the whole climb. The terrain (between Camp 3 and 4 and the ice wall above) is extremely difficult in parts

– and all this at between 5500 and 7000m above sea level!

All the camps will now have to be reoccupied and the fixed ropes (almost 2000m of them) need to be checked in case avalanches might have damaged them. But the weather still is not good enough. The snowflakes are still dancing outside. We are still here lying in damp sleeping bags, trying to keep our fingers warm and write a few more lines.

I hope everyone is well at home. Here, we are sleeping up to sixteen hours a day, so I can make up for all the sleep I missed over the winter.

We don't know when this letter will be posted. We will only be able to send it down when everything is back to normal. A mail runner will then take it to Gilgit.

We are always happy to hear from home.

Love,

Reinhold and Günther

Another snowy night was followed by a bright, sunny morning. To the east it was now clear. To the west a bank of cloud had rolled in. We were still at the ice cave, the space in front cleared of snow.

Günther sat on an inflatable mattress next to me outside the tent and cooked. We were enjoying the warm sun and the play of the clouds below us.

'Do you think it will hold?' Günther asked.

'I don't like this weather.'

There was too much cloud. They formed out of nothing, swirling and merging, the sun turning them all the colours of the rainbow before they again dispersed into nothing.

'The others are coming tomorrow,' Günther said.

'Only if the weather holds.'

'The weather report is good, you said so yesterday.'

'That doesn't mean the weather is going to be good.'

The next day – the weather was indeed better – the others came up. Felix arrived at Camp 3 at midday. He was first, as usual. He sat down on an air bed and drank tea. Peter and Gerhard had stayed at Camp 2. They arrived later. Felix pulled a nylon bag with letters in it out of his rucksack. 'Post for you guys, and Karl's plan of attack,' he said dryly. I read the letters first, then studied the OUTLINE PLAN (*see* pages 138 and 139 for abbreviations).

Day 1 (11.6.70)
Reinhold Messner + Günther Messner are at C3
Kuen + Scholz + Baur BC → C3
WC occupied by Saler + Mändl + Haim + Vogler
BC ' C2 Kühn + Kroh
C1 Raab + 9 HP C1 → C2 → C1

Day 2 (12.6.70)
C3 rest day; consolidate camp
2 HP (Sepp + Ibadat) C1 → C3, led by Kroh
(Kroh → C2)
2 HP from BC → C1 (9 HP). Winkler BC → C2

Day 3 (13.6.70)
R. M. + G. M. + Kuen + Scholz → C4
2 HP (Sepp + Ibadat) rest day at C3
2 HP (Arab Khan + Ali Madad) with Kroh C1 → C3
Anderl + W. Bitterling BC → C1
C2 Kühn + Winkler
C1 Raab with 9 HP C1 → C2 → C1
2 HP from BC stay at C1 (9 in all) → Isa + Valayat

Day 4 (14.6.70)
R. M. + G. M. + Ku. + Sch. consolidate C4 / recce C5
C3 → C4 → C3 Saler + Mändl + Haim + 4 HP
C3 → C4 Baur
WC occupied by Kühn + Vogler + Winkler
C1 → C2 Anderl + Raab + 2 HP (Isa + Valayat)
C1 W.Bi. → BC → C1 2 HP, C1 occupied by 9 HP

Day 5 (15.6.70)
R. M. + G. M. + Ku. + Sch. C4 → C5, establish and consolidate
C3 → C4 → C3 Kroh with 4 HP
C3 → C4 Mändl + Saler + Haim
WC still occupied by Kühn, Vogler, Winkler – one of them to fetch the 2 HP up from C2!
C2 Anderl + Raab
C1 W.Bi.

Day 6 (16.6.70)
C4 rest day for R. M. + Ku. + Sch. + Mändl + Baur
Haim + G. M. + Saler fix the MC (1st part) from C5
C3 → C4 → C3 4 HP with Kühn or Kroh
WC 2HP + Vogler
C2 Anderl + Raab
C1 W.Bi.

Day 7 (17.6.70)
C5 Haim + G. M. + Saler fix 2nd part of MC. Possible support from some of those at C4 (R. M., Sch., Ku., Mä., Baur?)
C3 → C4 → C3 4HP with Kroh or Kühn or Vogler.

Day 8 (18.6.70)
C5 Haim + G. M. + Saler fix 3rd part of MC and descend in the evening to C4
C4 → C5 R. M. + Ku. + Sch. + Mä. + Baur, sleep there on oxygen until midnight and set off at 1 o'clock (19th June full moon) in 2 teams for the summit.

1st Summit team: Reinhold Messner + P. Scholz
2nd Summit team: Kuen + Mändl + Baur (camera)
Substitute for Kuen: Haim
        for Mändl: Saler or G. M.
        for Baur: Winkler

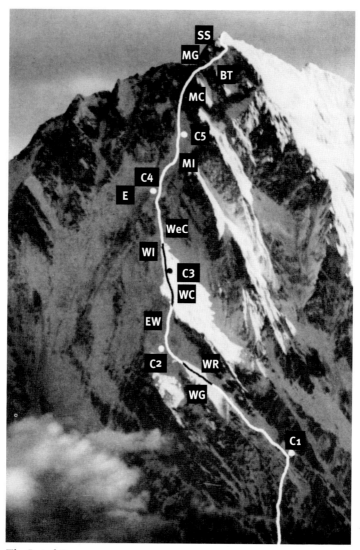

The Rupal Face.

C1 to C5 = camps, WG = Wieland Glacier, WR = Wieland Rocks, EW = Ice Wall, WC = Winch Camp, WI = Welzenbach Icefield, WeC = Welzenbach Couloir, E = Ice Bulge, MI = Merkl Icefield, MC = Merkl Couloir, BT = Big Traverse, MG = Merkl Gap, SS = South Shoulder.

After the two named teams have reached the summit, further participants may follow as long as there is no risk of bad weather and the teams coming down do not require the help of the others to descend.

C	=	Camp	HP	=	High-altitude Porters
BC	=	Base Camp	MC	=	Merkl Couloir
WC	=	Winch Camp			

I had read some time earlier that Karl Herrligkoffer did not hold the principles of leadership in very high regard. Then this plan arrived, which I was supposed to approve. According to the plan, Peter Scholz and I were to have been the first team to go for the summit, with Felix Kuen, Gert Mändl and Gerhard as the second. My brother Günther and Hans Saler, with Werner Haim, were meant to spend three consecutive days fixing the Merkl Couloir. It would not only be three days of hard labour in the Death Zone, it would actually be more strenuous than going for the summit.

Günther now wanted to see the battle plan. I gave him the sheets of paper and, tried to placate him: 'No one should be expected to do the impossible. An assault plan must be reasonable. If someone orders you to fix ropes all the way up the Merkl Couloir he is denying you the chance to summit. It's much easier to go to the top than to spend three days in a row going up and down between 7200m and 7800m' I said. Günther read on.

'Karl has obviously only spoken to part of the team. Now he's relying on you approving his plan. He hasn't even asked me. He doesn't like it when anyone interferes with his plans,' Günther remarked after he had finished reading.

'Him down there, he thinks a bit like a field marshall before the battle,' I agreed angrily.

'But since our Field Marshall is unwell, the battle plan is a sick one, too.' I shared Günther's irony. If an expedition

Descending to Camp 3 in poor conditions.

leader stipulates that one man spends three consecutive days fixing the Merkl Couloir so the well-rested summit team can go up the fixed ropes to the top and the guy simply decides to go for the summit first, then no one can criticize him. If he gives unreasonable orders he has no right to expect reasonable reactions. It can't be right. And no one can work out a reasonable plan for a summit assault if they have never even been this high before.

The good weather did not even last two days and the latest change in conditions threw both the summit assault and the plan into disarray, or rather buried them in the snow. We radioed down to Base Camp and placed an order for cranberries, egg nog, beer and dried fruit but none of these delicacies were available at any of the lower camps. Or was it that the people at Base Camp simply did not want to part with them? I didn't know. It was only much later that these little luxuries, or what remained of them, were discovered at Camp 1 and at Base Camp. All we wanted to do was to stock up for a long spell of bad weather. We now knew what tasted best in the high camps, when stormbound or when we had to set off at one in the morning. When you are living at altitude for days on end, eating and drinking should be a pleasure at least.

It was snowing again. Felix stood at the edge of the campsite, shovel in hand, cursing softly to himself. Günther and Gerhard were lying next to me in the tent.

'This snow is getting on my nerves,' Günther said.

'Me too!'

'New snow, storms, always the same. The sleeping bags are wet. It's enough to put you off camping for life.'

'Let's go down,' I suggested.

'Better to wait a bit,' said Gerhard.

'It's been like this for ten days now.'

'Felix, do you want to go down?' one of us asked after a while. It was an attempt to talk to Felix.

'In this weather it would be stupid to stay here.' Felix Kuen was right about that, at least.

What really annoyed me about Felix Kuen's attitude was his apathy with regard to Herrligkoffer's strategy, apathy that bordered on subservience. Or was it that he, a soldier, despised us for our anti-war 'conscientious objector' stance? At any rate, he did not want to talk to us about it.

Felix knew that The Herrligkoffer Battle Plan gave him a good chance of reaching the summit. That was really all he wanted. The way the logistics worked, it even gave him some hope that he might go right to the front of the queue. First on the summit – every climber's dream.

As a soldier, Felix Kuen knew that subordination was a condition of service. He was also well aware that on this expedition blind obedience was rewarded. Kuen could only win his personal 'Battle for the Summit of Nanga Parbat' if Herrligkoffer was with him, not against him. So he regarded Karl as a capable expedition leader and did what was expected of him: he obeyed orders. Kuen's attitude disturbed my sense of self-determination.

Chapter VIII

Worlds Apart

The Rupal Face.

The leader of an expedition must have authority and a
talent for cool calculation. I would compare him to a
military leader, a General perhaps, who drafts the battle
plan. He directs, coordinates and calls off the attack
from the command post but does not actually go over
the top with his troops and lead the frontline charge on
the enemy trenches himself. As far as I am aware, a
General always has a general staff officer at his side, a
man well-versed in military matters, who advises him
and whose word carries great weight. Dr Herrligkoffer
always had a mountaineering adviser with him. In our
case this was Michl Anderl from Bad Tölz.

Felix Kuen

View of the upper part of the South-East Buttress.

That wonderful Main Summit. And beneath it – a
single, unbroken precipice of 5000m – the South
Buttress. It makes you feel so tiny. In spite of my
reluctance to use terms like 'overwhelming' and
'immense', here they really do apply, with no
exaggeration whatsoever.

Hubert Ruths, 1938

The South Face is a mountain wall seamed with
vertical cliffs. Even to attempt it would be suicide.

Hermann Buhl

Doubts About the Leadership

Herrligkoffer: 'I was now sufficiently aware of the mountaineering problems presented by the Rupal Flank. I knew where the individual camps had to be placed, that we could best supply the acclimatization camp by using the drag lift set-up on the Wieland Ice Wall and that we needed to relocate Camp 2 nearer to the bottom lift station in order to make the job of attaching the plastic barrels to the 300m drag line easier to do from close by the camp. The plan was to place Camp 4 higher up the mountain, at the glacier on the lower Merkl Icefield. The last camp before the summit would then be a bivouac tent pitched at 7350m at the start of the Merkl Couloir.'

Although the expedition leader was operating on the Rupal Face for the fourth time now, the logistical problems of the task he had set himself remained alien to him, even if he often maintained that the opposite was true. His plans were made in whispered conversations with his confidantes. Yes, Herrligkoffer did take advice, even from me. In this way at least a kind of rapprochement existed between us; but the relationship was never based on mutual trust.

I was always talking to Karl, on the radio and later at Base Camp. We discussed a possible new strategy for a summit push and variations on the route. But other expedition members were also sharing their thoughts on the various scenarios for the crucial days with the expedition leader and since these conversations never took place with the group as a whole the impression arose that secret agreements had been made and that cliquism was at work. For his part, Felix Kuen remained to the last Herrligkoffer's trusty and most obedient vassal.

Kuen: 'The often-heard criticism that Herrligkoffer had too little experience as a mountaineering leader is something that I find wrong. The final judgement must be made by the team working up on the mountain pushing the route to the summit. They assess the dangers and weigh the possibilities but they need an organizer down at Base Camp to provide the crucial umbilical cord on which they hang.'

Felix was right about this. Without a functioning supply chain, any classic Himalayan expedition would soon be over. We were a part of a cumbersome apparatus that functioned like a snow plough, with the lead team pushing the route out in front, a number of helpers lower down and, right at the back, one man, the strategist, whose job it was to steer the whole enterprise in a sensible manner.

Back to Base Camp

Camp 2. Jürgen was clearing snow, Gine was looking out of the tent. Felix, Günther and I had just arrived. Hermann, as always, helpful and obliging, gave us tea from his thermos flask. We all liked him a lot.

Günther and I had decided to go back down. Only Peter and Gerhard stayed up at Camp 3. We got tea at the Winch Camp. Werner and Gert, who were keeping it occupied, were also thinking about descending but they said they would wait one more day. The next day they received the order from below to stay up there and haul loads. Even though the storm continued unabated they still did their duty. Finally, they came down too in spite of the order to stay where they were.

There was now a danger of avalanches. After a short rest the three of us set off again. The first man broke trail through the virgin snow; the other two followed at equal intervals. It was snowing and the fixed ropes were frozen

Günther Messner during the descent to Base Camp.

hard in the snow and had to be prised free, section by section. Sometimes, when they were buried too deeply in the snow, it was impossible to pull them out and we often sank in up to our knees trying. Still, we stumbled on down, like drunks. The amount of new snow was worrying; progress was tiring and slow.

Elmar was at Camp 1. He fed us like he always did. Felix, Günther and I then continued our descent, all the way back down to Base Camp. The others followed next day. The days at the foot of the Face were spent resting and getting cleaned up. It did us all good. We filled the time bathing in the stream, writing, taking photographs, playing games and having long, lively discussions.

Günther wrote his letters. He sat alone on a big rock a little way above Base Camp, writing. Now and then, he would

147

Descending after the period of bad weather.

gaze into space, the writing pad balanced on his knees, as if deep in thought. This was his last letter:

Rupal Valley, Tap Alpe, 15.6.1970

Dear Parents,

Dear Brothers and Sister,

Today we have been on the mountain for exactly a month. On 15.5 we established our main camp here at Tap Alpe. A lot has happened and changed in the meantime. The snow has melted and things are now looking green at Tap Alpe, the meadows are full of flowers: it looks a bit like an English garden. Half-wild herds of yaks romp about in this wild and romantic, basin-shaped high valley, while half-starved horses recover from the hard winter. Such contrasts!

148

I am sitting quite high above Base Camp with a view out over the whole valley. The Alpe itself is a meadow that is almost as flat as a table. In the middle there is a wood. The storms and avalanches have left their mark here, too, with every second tree defoliated and withered. In the evenings the porters often bring us five or six of these dead trees to make a huge bonfire. (Our mountain campfires at home are a joke by comparison!)

To the north, directly above us, is the Rupal Flank – 4500m to the summit. It is unbelievably impressive. Two huge moraines border Tap Alpe to the east and west. To the South, Rupal Peak dominates the valley. It is a coveted objective for our 'amateur mountaineers'; so far, however, they have not reached the summit! Our Base Camp lies roughly in the north-west corner of the corrie, next to two freshwater springs, about five minutes away. Base Camp consists of about fifteen tents, including accommodation for the porters, the camp kitchen, the mess tent and the leader's tent. Everything is neatly fenced off and in the middle of the circle there is a pole with the German and Pakistani flags. Everyone has his own tent where, if it rains or snows, he can write, read and sleep and where he can keep his personal belongings. Reinhold and I are sharing a three-man tent. It's really comfortable. We've got inflatable mattresses and sleeping bags too, of course, and no one dictates to us how we have to organize our own tents.

That was a brief insight into life at Base Camp, the mother camp that supplies all our exposed and advanced high camps. So why am I writing you a letter today from the main camp when the letter from Camp 3 has not even gone off yet? Well, for ten days now all hell has been let loose here – not in the team, they have worked together in an exemplary and comradely way; no, our problem is the weather. Since 3.6. it has been snowing and storming practically without a break. In the high camps there are great quantities of new snow (a metre or more!) every day. Avalanches thunder down the endless steep flanks of the mountain. It's good to know that so far Reinhold and I have located all the sites for the camps ourselves and checked them all for avalanche danger before pitching the tents. Camp 1 is under a big protruding rock; Camp 2 beneath a 20m high, vertical line of seracs whose upper part forms a ridge that splits the avalanches and funnels them down to the left and right of the camp. Camp 3 is our famous Ice Dome, again safe from avalanches. Camp 4 is as yet unoccupied (we reached it on 3.6.70 but bad weather forced a retreat).

The Face is exceptionally dangerous and malicious with new snow on it. If there is a risk of avalanche there is no climbing or carrying done, even in fine weather. In the space of twelve days, all the high camps have been vacated and the team has returned to Base Camp. As you will gather from the other letter I wrote, Reinhold and I spent ten full days at Camp 3 in a snowstorm waiting for better weather. We only stayed so long because the descent would have been too risky.

On 10.6. it was again a more or less sunny, windless day. The new snow had either gone or it had consolidated and during the course of the day the rest of the team, who had been at Base Camp since 5.6., went back up to the high camps. Renewed hope and plenty of impetus seemed to have ushered in a new period in the life of the expedition. On 11.6. Reinhold and I wanted to go up to Camp 4 and finally locate a good, safe site on the lower edge of the Merkl Icefield to establish a camp. The food we had carted up on 3.6. would have lasted for two to three days, at which point the others would be up with additional supplies, but in the morning we were greetd by hailstones and a black cloud that enveloped Nanga like a wreath so we quickly crawled back into the tent. At eight o'clock all hell broke loose again. We were annoyed. Firstly, we would soon have spent fourteen full days at Camp 3 at 6000m; secondly, we felt like we really needed some exercise. So we decided that if the weather really hadn't improved by 12.6 or at the very latest 13.6 we would go down. Thanks to good acclimatization we descended to Base Camp in just a few hours on 13.6. The weather report from Peschawar was still bad and on 14.6. the rest of the team (nine men) cleared the high camps (food supplies had run short again, as the high-altitude porters had been unable to do any real carries since about 3.6.).

Today, 15.6., we are all (18 sahibs, 15 porters and the 25 year-old liaison officer) assembled here at Base Camp. The cloudbase is down to Tap Alpe and there are frequent light showers. Up on the Rupal Flank the avalanches thunder down. As you can imagine, the mood is rather depressed, even if not everyone shows it. Hopes of reaching the summit are fading in this lousy weather and some are saying that there's no sense in continuing.

There are some of us here who do not want to give up in any circumstances; we reckon it is cheaper to stay here than to come back again. If the worst comes to the worst, we would like to stay until 15.7. as experience has shown that the monsoon time brings with it a period of fine weather! Unfortunately, we are running short of food; we are already talking about rationing it.

Today, for example, we bought a young yak for 200 rupees, which we are going to consume during the next period of bad weather. We also want to buy eggs, flour, potatoes and rice from the farmers and cook 'Rupalese' to save the valuable food we brought with us for the high camps. By doing this we should be able to prevent the food running out suddenly. We still have a surfeit of canned vegetables and there are huge quantities of rhubarb to be found here.

As I write, our porters are busy with some of the local farmers, trying to catch the young ox that we are going to roast on a spit in the next few days. They are chasing after the semi-wild beast like a bunch of stone-age men!

Everyone is fit and well. All apart from our youngest, Peter Vogler, who is seriously ill. Suffering terribly, he managed to

151

drag himself back down from Winch Camp to Base. The diagnosis is pleurisy. Reinhold and I are fine, although (or maybe because) we have lost weight and our noses are peeling again.

The mail runner comes every four or five days. A fit little farmer from Tarshing, he brings the post and eggs. The following day he rides or drives the Jeep back to Gilgit. Apparently the Gilgit road has now been repaired again. On the approach march it was closed to traffic, which was why we had to walk. So tomorrow he will be going back to Gilgit with about twenty of our letters, most of them written while we were stormbound at Camp 3.

It must be the school holidays at home now and we are curious to know where you will all be when we get home. Have Helmuth, Erich and Waltraud received our letters yet? The postal service is a bit slow and I think some letters do go missing.

The ox has now been slaughtered and we are looking forward to liver and lungs and to kebabs with lots of vegetables. You can write to us until the end of June, as we will still get post in Gilgit, or even in Rawalpindi. How long the return journey will last depends on the weather, although it will be six days at least from Base Camp.

Looking forward to seeing you all again,
Günther and Reinhold

It was night. At Base Camp, the tents stood like dark wedges silhouetted against the sky. A little further off a fire was burning. A few people stood around it talking. Sparks floated in the air. A face appeared in the glow of the burning logs. The beard was dishevelled, the skin on the cheeks and nose broken and scabbed. The man gazed into the fire, deep in thought. It was Hans. I went over to join him.

Hans Saler was one of the best climbers on the team. It was he who had brought the sick Peter down from Winch Camp to Base. He had saved the life of one of the porters

152

when he slipped and fell on the way up to Camp 2. Hans did not say much. He had been all over the place, all over the world. Hans Saler had become a kind of nomad. He wrote poems and stories.

We had now been on the mountain for exactly one month. Hans had grown used to the feeling of hopelessness and always seemed to find something positive about the whole thing. We no longer had to persuade ourselves that it would go, but who – apart from us – still believed there was a chance of getting to the summit? Had Karl already secretly given up? If only we knew what he was thinking.

The fire had died down, glowing embers and charcoal were all that was left. We chatted.

'Karl is just exploiting us,' someone said.

'We stick our necks out; he makes sure we've got what we need,' Hans remarked.

'What he needs, you mean.'

'Yes, but let's face it, he's still the one who organized the expedition,' came the reply.

There are expedition leaders who speak to their team every day; who climb themselves, taking their turn out at the front; who share the best things with their team: the risks, the route finding, the hopes and the disappointments. They are part of the team. A good leader will make himself useful during the expedition, not just during the preparation and evaluation phases.

'We are not allowed to talk about our adventures afterwards, because we have signed a restrictive contract,' Hans said.

'The idea is that none of the team should adopt a different stance to Karl.'

'The facts would not be pleasant for him,' I said and they all laughed.

'He could even claim he had been to the summit!'

'In actual fact, lots of German-speaking people believe that Herrligkoffer is a great mountaineer.'

153

'No! Surely not?'

'And we're not allowed to put the record straight?'

'Tough luck, eh?', Hans commented.

In the evenings we often sat around the fire chatting to each other. Karl rarely joined us. The discussions often lasted until late into the night and the next morning we would have a lie in. After all, we were not missing anything.

It was a bright, sunny morning. The Rupal Face was almost cloud free. Günther stood in front of the yellow tent and looked at his watch; it was 9:15. He looked up at the Rupal Face and took a photo, then he threw his towel over his shoulder and disappeared off to have a wash. I followed him.

We stopped at the porters' cooking area. From the way they smiled it was obvious that the Hunzas liked us. The offered us chapattis, fresh from the fire, and tea. After the meal we thanked them and wandered along the narrow path to the watering place, about 200m away from the main camp. A lot of laughing went on there and we would spend hours washing our clothes and ourselves. On the mountain, by contrast, we never even brushed our teeth.

Base Camp looked almost deserted. I stood by the tent and looked around. Karl went past. There was no spring in his step, no enthusiasm. He looked tired: deep folds in his face; his hair white; his eyes had lost their shine; a tragic figure. He paced restlessly up and down the campsite like a man who can see no way out. In such moments, whenever we happened to bump into each other, there was always a little embarrassed smile, but rarely any more than that.

His body bent, his gait slow and ponderous, Karl made his way back to his tent. Was he sick again? His posture made you think of failed expeditions; of ill fortune, intrigue and criticism; of the embarrassing questions posed by journalists when they sense a scandal; and of the same old recycled excuses. I felt sorry for him sometimes. I wanted to understand him but could not see behind the mask he wore.

154

Günther Messner at Base Camp.

Karl did liven up once, and once only. It happened quite suddenly. He was standing in the middle of the team and started talking about Hermann Buhl. He had watched Buhl through his binoculars as he pushed the route up the Rakhiot Ice Face, climbing quickly, far ahead of the 'Hunza Tigers'. 'The way that man Buhl broke trail, fixing ropes as he went!' He must have impressed Karl so much that the mere memory of it made him wish that he, too, could be as skilful as

155

Buhl. His dream was not just to be here but to lead the climb, but in the end it was he who had brought Buhl into the team and he who had sent him ahead. Yet the idea of going right to the top, of reaching the summit himself, still gnawed away at him. *Herligkoffer was still enthusiastic about what happened high up the mountain, even if he was just watching events unfold through a telescope at Base Camp.*

As he watched, it was not Buhl or Welzenbach he was thinking about, but Merkl, his brother. It was his ideal that drove him; the image of Willy Merkl leading his team to storm the summit... In such moments he perhaps saw himself up there in the lead, breaking trail, and everything merged into one: the mountain, the brother and he. All his emotions were focused on the summit, all hopes directed towards this one objective.

So was Karl ill or was he just a man at odds with himself? Did he realize that it was too late for him to fulfil his summit dream? He had lived for this moment of total identification for 36 years; he had spared neither expense nor effort (the preparation for his expeditions had taken months and years) and now he was disappointed. For he knew now that a satisfactory ending for himself could only be achieved if he had the ability to do the climb. Unfortunately this was not possible for him; in fact, the chances were looking slim for the whole expedition and most of the team were already silently resigned to the fact.

Excursion to Heran Peak

While everyone at Base Camp was waiting for better weather, Günther and I made a long, somewhat secretive excursion to climb Heran Peak. (Karl Herrligkoffer calls the mountain Shaigiri Peak.)

The South East Face of Nanga Parbat with Heran Peak in the background.

Herrligkoffer: 'In the late afternoon of 16th June, the Messner brothers sneaked out of Base Camp with Raab and von Kienlin to "take a look" at Shaigiri. Raab came back to Base a short time later. The other three returned the following day, Reinhold and Günther Messner having made the first ascent of Shaigiri Peak (5950m).'

Peter was lying in his tent. He had recovered from the pleurisy and now had to wrap up warm and rest. He wanted to be back up on the mountain in a few days; I could see it in his eyes.

Günther sat next to him on a cushion and talked about our first ascent of Heran Peak. 'In the last few weeks we could often see Heran Peak from Camp 3 – when it was not snowing, that is. It looked tempting, and not all that difficult. We just did not know the name of the peak or how high it was.

157

But for us one thing was for sure – it was still unclimbed. And so it was that this six-thousander high up at the head of the Rupal Valley suddenly became our objective. We agreed that we would use a day of fine weather at Base Camp to sneak off surreptitiously (Karl must not know what our actual objective was), recce the mountain and, if possible, climb it.

'We set off yesterday about four in the afternoon. Elmar followed us as far as the bridge; about two hours' walk from here. Unfortunately he was wearing training shoes, the low-cut ones we only ever wear at Base Camp. When it started raining we waited under a rocky overhang. Later on we found a hut in a burnt down hamlet. It was the last remaining dwelling of what was once a high alpine settlement and had been spared for some reason. It was full of cow muck and very cramped but at least it had a solid roof and was not too uncomfortable. Reinhold cleared the hut out and we fetched some wood, some of which was half-burned. There wasn't much talking. Inside we built benches and a fireplace. Night was falling as we sat in front of the fire. We ate what we had with us: bread and cheese, and a tin of fruit. We laughed a lot.

'The rain stopped about nine o'clock and Elmar set off home, looking a little sorry for himself. He had the wrong shoes on. We would have liked to have him accompany us; we were very fond of Elmar.

'We carried on by the light of the moon, slowly but steadily. It was all about endurance. It wasn't always easy to find the way in the dark. Later we turned off into a side valley. At first we used a lateral moraine as the easiest way of gaining height but this soon became impossible to negotiate as the moon had now disappeared behind Rupal Peak and its reflection from the Rupal Face and the Mazeno Ridge gave little light. So we scrambled back down onto the glacier through a sea of rocks and potholes. Reinhold was out in front, searching for the best way between the crevasses.

On the summit ridge of Heran Peak. The Middle Summit is in the foreground.

Max and I followed a few hundred metres behind. We wanted to turn back but Reinhold ignored our shouts and carried on. From time to time he used his torch to light the way for us.

'On the other side of the glacier the going got easier, first over rocks, then across avalanche debris and finally across the glacier again. Whenever we sank into wet snow, which did not happen very often, we looked around for hard-packed snow to walk on to save our strength.

'We reached the foot of a gully and thought long and hard about what to do. Wasting little time on words, Reinhold set off climbing. We had to let him get on with it; it wasn't even midnight yet. Further up, below a steep step in the gully, he stopped and waited for us. Max was very tired and wanted to rest. His toes were freezing, too. Reinhold left him his rucksack and bivi bag with instructions to wrap himself up and wait until the morning sun appeared and warmed him up. Reinhold and I then kicked steps up the last steep snow slopes leading to the ridge. The snow was hard packed in places and we took turns breaking trail. Up near the ridge we stopped to take photographs in all directions. Once, we even got a brief glimpse of the top of Nanga Parbat, otherwise everything was in cloud.

'Seven o'clock or thereabouts and we were standing on a summit. At first we thought it was the real one but then the clouds parted and we saw an even higher one so we carried on. The mist was getting thicker. The climbing was quite exciting, and not easy either. We took it slowly, up snow-covered rock pinnacles and a few steep sections on the ridge, roped up and belaying each other on the awkward bits. Things soon started to flatten out and then we really were on the summit. We only noticed it when the cloud lifted for a moment.

'It had started snowing again so we kept it brief: just a handshake and two summit photos. We looked at the watch; it was late afternoon, too late to hang about waiting for better visibility. The altimetre read 6022m. Our original plan was to down-climb the route, and to do it as fast as possible, as Max was waiting for us somewhere below, but on the way back to the subsidiary summit we chanced across a broad gully. I don't know why, but the cloud lifted suddenly, just for a short time, and we agreed that climbing straight down the gully was a better option. We dropped into the gully, feeling pleased with ourselves, and then thought of Max, who was waiting for us further down. So we traversed across left to the point at which we had left him.

'But Max was not there. The rucksack was lying on a rock with the bivi bag. There was a note written in the snow: "Went up after you". He must have set off shortly after sunrise then. At first we just shouted, then Reinhold climbed back up a bit. Max's footsteps were clearly visible in the snow.

'Suddenly Max appeared, heading down towards us. He was tired and stumbled along, leaning heavily on his ski poles. He had been to the middle summit on his own.

160

Günther Messner and Max von Kienlin on Heran Peak.

'We walked back in rain and snow. We arrived back here shortly after four in the afternoon, twenty-four hours after we had set off.'

Back at Base Camp, the reception was frosty. It was as if we had done something wrong.

Karl never did bother to ask us where we had been. We were told he had cursed us because we went off on our own, even though he had given our little excursion his approval the day before. Some of the others asked him if they could go and do the second ascent but their requests were turned down. Herrligkoffer thought it would be stupid, not worth the effort, a waste of energy. As if hanging around at Base Camp made any sense. What did this man have planned? We had no idea. Who could guess what he was thinking?

Chapter IX

Intrigue or Misunderstanding?

Reinhold and Günther Messner climbing as a team.

And then we see the Rupal Face, a single, compact 4500m precipice. Geologists find it astonishing that the Face is so uniform in appearance despite the huge vertical distance.

Günther Oskar Dyhrenfurth

*Reinhold Messner on
Nanga Parbat in 1970.*

There were some evenings when Herrligkoffer really
livened up. When he came into the mess tent, pulled
up a crate, opened a can of beer and played cards it
was as if he really did belong to the team. Sometimes
he would come out of his shell and tell stories about
earlier expeditions and every time he looked at me I
had a strange mixture of feelings: sympathy for his
illness and high esteem for his single-mindedness.
Suppressed anger then gave way to understanding –
perhaps he wasn't really as bad as he seemed,
perhaps he was just incapable of being any different.
He often seemed about to say something important
but then the conversation would dry up unexpectedly
and suddenly he would disappear. I still did not
know how far he trusted us and whether it was right
for us to trust him. It was probably for this reason
that tensions existed between him and some of the
team. Every time the conversation got a bit loud and
boisterous, I found myself involuntarily addressing
him with the formal 'Sie'.

Reinhold Messner

Life at Base Camp

Evening at Base Camp. Günther and I lay in our sleeping bags in the tent writing our diaries.

'We should really be getting some sleep now. If the weather is better tomorrow we'll be going back up,' I said.

'What a day! My first six-thousander.'

'You're really on top form.'

We heard Felix' voice outside: 'The summit is only 5908m high.' Günther laughed.

'As if that's going to change anything; it was still a first ascent.'

Some of our companions were standing outside our tent talking about the height of Heran Peak. One of them was so loud you could hear him right across the campsite.

No one knew the exact height of Heran Peak – apart from Karl, who had a big map of the Nanga Parbat region that he didn't like showing us.

During the night, Felix, Peter, Gert and Hermann set off for Rupal Peak, a 5000m summit directly opposite Nanga Parbat. They returned at midday the following day. Jürgen was busy taking advertising shots for an apple sauce company. Perched on a round container was a box with the label:

SIGI-LÖW GEDÄCHTNIS-EXPEDITION [memorial expedition]
8 MÜNCHEN 25, WEST GERMANY
LEITER [leader]: DR. HERRLIGKOFFER

Jürgen snapped away, equipped with camera and tripod and surrounded by a group of climbers spooning apple sauce straight from the tin. Jürgen was taking it all very seriously. He was the only one working and not eating. He didn't say that the others should actually eat the stuff, just that they should pretend to. He checked his settings, adjusted the focus and clicked the shutter mechanism. Sometimes he would stop, look and wipe the sweat from his brow. You could tell immediately that he was really into his work. Jürgen was an excellent photographer, he could even work without us noticing. All in all, he was to take 400 advertising shots during the expedition.

The tin was now empty. Jürgen stowed his photo gear in the tent and came over to join us. We were now sitting outside Herrligkoffer's tent listening to the radio news on Deutsche Welle, the German World Service. We could hear the voice of the announcer, distorted but clear enough.

Just at that moment, Felix arrived at the leader's tent, fresh back from Rupal Peak. He said he had reached the summit ahead of the others and explained how he had crossed the glacier stream at the foot of the mountain – ahead of the others, of course.

'And make sure you bring them back!' Karl shouted from his tent as his assistant, Alice von Hobe, passed Jürgen a packet of dried fruit. It was the only one I saw during the whole expedition. Jürgen understood – he was to return the product as soon as he had taken the necessary advertising photos. In spite of everything, Jürgen remained calm. He did not seem in the least surprised by the tone of Herrligkoffer's instructions. After all, it wasn't the first time.

'Won't even get a tin of apple sauce out to do his advertising photos,' Karl grumbled. The thinly veiled criticism was too much even for Jürgen. At first, he just sat there, helpless. Then his eyes narrowed. What made him angry was the fact that it was the others, not him, who had eaten the apple sauce. He had only been doing his job and was now getting stick for it.

Scene at Base Camp. Hans Saler and Günther Messner tend to the fire.

It was all turning sour now. There was a feeling of help-lessness at Base Camp. The weather was bad again and spir-its were low.

This mood of hesitancy had been going on for three weeks now, and there was so much mistrust in the team. Some of the members had already given up their dreams of climbing Nanga Parbat by the Rupal Face. Our repeated failure to establish the top camp had drained most people's courage and will to succeed.

At that very moment, I was called over to Herrligkoffer's tent. I was even asked to take a seat. At first I couldn't understand what I had done to deserve such an honour. However, Karl was the same as ever. The episode with the apple sauce that had so annoyed Jürgen had not bothered Herligkoffer at all. It was obviously just a trivial incident and for him there was more at stake. Suddenly, Herrligkoffer got all personal with me.

'What are your thoughts on our situation?' he asked.

'It's not hopeless.'

'So what should we do?'

'I suggest we go back on the face once last time despite the bad weather. We go back up to Camp 3 and if the weather improves, carry on. If it stays bad, we dismantle the camps. We shouldn't wait around any more. Someone has to go up to Camp 3 anyway to get the cameras, the big film camera and the radio. They can't be left on the mountain.'

'Agreed.'

I liked Herrligkoffer when he spoke openly with me; when he, the organizer, talked to me as a climber. It was then that I could appreciate his leadership; after all, it was he who had got our expedition off the ground in the first place.

'How much time have we still got, Karl?' I asked him.

'The permit runs out on the seventh of June.'

'What happens if we're up in the Merkl Couloir and the weather's good?'

'I'll get it extended.'

'Okay.'

'When do you want to go back up?'

'This evening.'

'Who?'

'Whoever wants to. The lads who have just got back from Rupal Peak will be tired. They should rest up. I'll ask who wants to come with me. Günther will certainly want to, Werner too, as far as I know, and Elmar. He knows his way around Camp 1; he could stay there.'

'How many porters do you need?'

'As many as possible. We'll need to get the loads that are lying around up there from Camp 1 to Camp 2.'

'Will twelve be enough?'

' I reckon so, but I'll have to talk to the others about it.'

'Let me know.'

As I left his tent I felt relieved and suspicious at the same time. I felt suddenly constrained by responsibility. Herrligkoffer is approachable after all, I thought.

A while later all the crates in the mess tent were occupied as we laughed, chatted and teased each other. Everywhere there was movement. Someone poured hot water into our mugs. Everyone had something warm to eat and drink. 'Tomorrow we're off!' I said.

We agreed that Werner, Elmar, Günther and I should take the lead. The others would follow at daily intervals. No one asked why Herrligkoffer had made the decision so suddenly.

Günther and I packed our gear. Then we decided to write one last letter home together. Günther began:

Rupal Valley, Base Camp, 18 June 1970

All the sitting around doing nothing surrounded by five and six thousand metre peaks finally became unbearable. Nanga was still shrouded in cloud. At five in the evening, Reinhold, our expedition guest Max von Kienlin and I set off up the head of the Rupal Valley. We waited out a short thunderstorm in a shepherd's hut and at nine stomped off again by the light of the moon and headed left up into a wild and unexplored glacial valley, where we crossed a huge moraine.

'Günther, you need to get changed, and you still haven't packed your sack,' I interrupted.

I finished the letter off:

About midnight we were standing beneath a steep gully. I thought about it and then started climbing – and by a lucky coincidence it turned out to be the easiest route to the top of Heran Peak. Max gave up at four o'clock (at 5000m). We carried on climbing, got to the ridge and, about seven, reached the Middle Summit (5800m). Huge cornices, and fantastic views (even of Nanga!). The ridge to the Main Summit was hard so the rope came out of the rucksack. At nine o'clock we were there, in cloud and spindrift – but happy with our first ascent. The altimeter read 6022m. Max got as far as the Middle Summit. His joy knows no bounds!

The Final Assault

Elmar and Werner were saying their goodbyes. There was a certain finality to their gestures. Günther and I were still busy with our rucksacks; we did not want to forget anything important.

We saw the other members of the team standing around, singly and in little groups, scepticism written all over their faces. They were having their doubts. It seemed there were only a few of us who now believed we would be successful.

Günther and I went over to the mess tent for one last meal before saying goodbye to our friends. Somewhere, someone was laughing, very loud. It was like a showdown. Whoever it was, was regarding our departure more than critically, in direct contrast to Herrligkoffer, who seemed to have mustered new hope. Yes, Karl was there, too, saying his goodbyes. I wanted to tell him that we intended to give it our best shot and that we were going now. I left the camp with a feeling of gratitude.

Günther climbed over the fence that was strung around Base Camp. I followed, with one last look back. The camp was quiet, the tents glowing brightly in the early evening light. A lone figure came towards us. He waved, indicating that we should stop. It was Max. He always came out to say goodbye whenever anyone was going up the mountain. Originally designated as a kind of Base Camp administrator, he moved freely between the lower camps and took care of everyone. We were somehow dependent on him, although he wasn't really a climber in our sense of the term.

Finally, three of the porters – high-altitude Hunza porters – came running after us. They had always been very kind to us and now they, too, wanted to say goodbye. Handshakes all round and a 'Tike', their word for farewell.

Günther and I set off. We gained height quickly, following an indefinite little path between the rocks and clumps of grass. We had no trouble finding it; we had often used it before. Neither of us suspected that this would be the last time we would pass this way. After half an hour we were up on the big scree fan at the foot of the Rupal Face. The slopes of Rupal Peak opposite were bathed in the red light of the setting sun and Günther took some photographs.

The top half of our face was in cloud. Suddenly, it lifted for a moment and the summit became visible. Was this a sign, a signal that the moment for the summit push had finally come?

The avalanche debris at the foot of the face was soon negotiated; we now had dirty, furrowed snow on a hard, icy base to contend with. From time to time we stopped. Günther was quite calm, looking alternately at the ground and ahead as he climbed, the creaking of his steps in the snow like a musical accompaniment. Our rhythm was good. We encouraged each other. Rest. A silent nod of the head and on we went.

It was just getting dark as we arrived at Camp 1. Elmar, Werner and the twelve porters were already there. Elmar sorted out the loads for the following day's carry and I helped him weigh them. The night sky was clear and starry.

Werner, Günther, the twelve porters and I were on our feet again by one o'clock in the morning. The climb was going well; only one of the porters had so far given up.

We climbed as a convoy, tiny figures on the huge snow-field in the first light of morning. Crossing another area of avalanche debris, we reached the Wieland Rocks and traversed diagonally leftwards and up across steep slopes until we reached a section of deep, unconsolidated powder snow, the first we had encountered on this last push. It was too dangerous to continue so we clipped our rucksacks to the fixed ropes and turned back. We were down at Camp 1 before sunrise.

The next morning the porters went on ahead, since the trail to the rucksack depot had already been broken. Once

171

again, Werner, Günther and I stamped up the steep snow slopes to the Wieland Rocks. Yesterday's trail was now frozen hard and we made rapid progress. The climbing itself was no problem. Shortly before the Wieland Rocks we saw some of the porters racing down towards us. 'No rucksack,' one of them shouted. This was not good. Surely they weren't running away just because a few rucksacks were missing? They must have been swept away by an avalanche during the night. What now? It was crucial not to show any uncertainty. The Hunzas had to keep going; otherwise we might as well all give up now.

We finally found a couple of the rucksacks hanging on the fixed ropes, covered in snow, 2m lower than the previous day. The porters showed me three attachment rings that had been left hanging on the rope. The corresponding rucksacks were nowhere to be seen. I shared out the remaining rucksacks and sent three of the porters out in front without loads to help break trail.

Our group carried on climbing up the Wieland Rocks. We dragged the fixed rope out of the snow and kicked steps, the Hunzas following on behind. At the Wieland Glacier I sent the three porters without loads back down with instructions to start searching for the lost rucksacks at first light.

Herrligkoffer: 'After midnight they went up again and reached the fixed ropes on the Wieland Rocks but three of the rucksacks had been swept down the mountainside by a powder snow avalanche. They reached Camp 2, now completely buried, in the early morning hours and immediately set about digging it out.'

Our convoy was nearing the site of the old Camp 2. At first there was nothing to be seen of the tents. A single pole tip, as long as a finger, poked out of the snow. It looked bad, but by no means hopeless.

Straight away we all got down to work. Werner and Günther started shovelling snow, uncovering ropes, tins of food and cooking pots. The tents were ripped, the poles bent. I

Werner Heim at Camp 2.

repaired the tents as best I could, salvaging the bits that were still serviceable and sticking them all together with sticky tape. After several hours of hard work Camp 2 was again inhabitable and the food dumps had been uncovered. Even the weather seemed to be improving. At least the weather gods were showing some understanding.

The next morning the plan was to go up to Camp 3. Felix and Peter had arrived in the meantime; they would follow us up, climbing hard on our heels.

Conditions on the ice wall were good but breaking trail on the flat sections was very, very strenuous. There was nothing to be seen of the Winch Camp either and even the tents at Camp 3 were completely snowed in. Ours was bent and ripped in several places. It was one o'clock in the afternoon before we could move into the Ice Dome Camp.

It was certainly not easy to start all over again from the beginning. Although we were now acclimatized and well

Günther Messner at Camp 3.

used to the altitude, what use was that when we were wasting energy shovelling snow all day long? I hoped and prayed for a favourable weather report, for the wind to drop, for a little bit of luck.

That evening, the clouds finally lifted. Neither the mountain nor the weather could fool us now and we were desperate to push on and get higher.

Herrligkoffer: 'A period of fine weather is moving in. We intend to use the next few days for the first, and perhaps last, serious summit bid.'

Muttered words, groans and rustling – after a relatively quiet night, Camp 3 was slowly waking up. Outside, it was still dark. The candles we had lashed to the middle pole of the tent with leather straps were lit, but we couldn't be bothered getting up; not yet. In any case, we had agreed that Felix and Peter would take the lead on the next section of the route and break trail.

174

Günther got the stove going and started melting snow. It took a long time. Then he warmed up a tin of fruit. The stove hummed. All the entrances and the walls of the tent were encrusted with hoar frost. Felix stood by the tents and strapped on his crampons. He would be setting off soon, I thought.

Inside our tent, the warm tinned fruit was being passed around. Then we got dressed, rolled our sleeping bags up and strapped them to our rucksacks that were already packed full to bursting and lying in the entrance to the tent.

Finally, Günther, Gerhard and I crawled out of the tent, only to find Felix was still there, looking disparagingly at us. What was all that about? We all strapped our crampons on, each of us in his own little world. There was not much talking. The lights of the head torches bobbed and flickered in the moonlight. It was bitterly cold.

It was only then that Felix started climbing. Taking the lead, he traversed left, clipped his ascender to the fixed rope and started hauling himself up. Breaking trail was very strenuous; you could see it in his movements.

I set off up the ropes, following in Felix's tracks. After about a hundred metres I took over the hard work from him. Further down, Günther, Peter and Gerhard were now climbing, too. Günther also overtook Felix. The face was easy-angled here and the ropes were buried beneath a blanket of new snow. It was a hellish job to pull them free.

We all traversed left across a snow rib to gain some rocks and continued up to a couloir, one after the other, like a family of geese, tiny circles of light at the edge of a dark precipice. The ropes that Peter and Felix had fixed on this section weeks ago were undamaged; even the anchor points were in good order. Now, however, the face was getting steeper and all the snow had slid off the smooth surface of hard ice.

We were soon standing on blue-green ice peppered with little air bubbles. I kicked my crampons hard into the ice; only the tips of the two front points bit in as I led off diagonally leftwards up the smooth sheet of ice. The exposure was tremendous. Stripped of snow, the face seemed steeper and everything looked much more dangerous and difficult, the climbing bold and run out.

I ground to a halt and waited at the big, vertical band of seracs, where the rope ladders we had left in place a few weeks ago had been blown away by the high winds. Günther followed the pitch, then Felix. We were unsure of what to do. The first time up here, Peter had cracked the problem of this ice wall; he was a steady ice climber and I wanted to hand him the lead again, but Peter and Gerhard were not here yet. What should we do? Felix was grumbling again about them being late. I couldn't understand it. This constant petty jealousy was something I absolutely detested. It annoyed me so much that I led off and climbed the vertical ice step as fast as I could while Günther belayed. This was extreme ice climbing at 6600m above sea level – the hardest pitch on the Rupal Face. Everyone found this section hard, strenuous and strength-sapping to varying degrees, depending on the weight of their rucksack.

Later on, Peter and Felix pitched a lightweight Hiebeler tent above the ice bulge and beneath a little incline. This meant their camp was in exactly the same location as the 1968 expedition's Camp 4. Günther and I pressed on to the bergschrund on the Merkl Icefield. And for good reason, too: we pitched our tent in the safest spot. Tucked beneath an ice overhang, it was not just safe from avalanches but also protected from the worst of the sunshine. We were going to be spending a few days in this tent and we wanted to be as comfortable as possible.

Finally I crawled into my sleeping bag to write up my diary.

Camp 4 (6600m), 23 June 1970

We've been lying in the tent for an hour now. It is in a kind of snow hole again. Peter and Felix have stayed further down, at the site of the old Camp 4. They are digging around looking for the old tents. Archaeology?

176

Günther Messner at Camp 4.

This morning we made fast time to the big serac band. I got there at seven, but the ladders were missing, which meant some extreme climbing and finally some exposed pulls on the fixed ropes. We found the stuff that was buried from the first attempt and then Günther and I pushed on to the first bergschrund on the Merkl Icefield.

Mist and spindrift have unfortunately frustrated our search for the ideal campsite but we soon managed to dig a hole in the bergschrund and pitch the tent and now we are ensconced. It is cold now and it is going to get colder during the night. Maybe Peter and Felix will come up and join us tomorrow.

Camp 4, 24 June 1970

At seven o'clock we were woken by Werner, Hans and Gert. They brought food and soap up from Camp 3. Last night it was so cold that we only managed to doze fitfully. Now we need to stock the camp and extend it.

Peter and Felix came up during the course of the afternoon and we had a brief conference. We all agree that ours is the best campsite, so they are going to pitch their tent in our hole, too. It is really safe from avalanches here and if we get a tarpaulin up from one of the lower camps to use as a sunshade Camp 4 would really be perfect. I think camps ought to be pleasant. When you are climbing at altitude, comfort is secondary only to safety and with a bit of effort I reckon you can always build yourself a nice little 'house' to live in!

So far Günther and I had found all the campsites, planned their layout and even pitched a lot of the tents ourselves. I found the job of locating the camps quite satisfying; indeed, I was realizing more and more that this was one of the key tasks in any expedition.

Into the Death Zone

It was still night, but in the first dim light of morning you could make out a set of tracks leading past an ice cliff to lose itself in avalanche debris above. Higher up, the tracks reappeared, zig-zagging up a steep slope and turning sharp right through a chaotic jumble of ice blocks before heading in a perfectly straight line up a wall of ice. This was the trail leading to Camp 5 that Günther and I had made on 25 June. Finally we were summit bound. At last we were approaching our objective.

Günther and I were now below the Merkl Couloir, chopping a little platform out of the ice below a protruding rock outcrop – the site for Camp 5. 'This will be the springboard for the summit push,' I said.

Job done, I climbed on a little way further, unable to contain my curiosity any longer. Excited now, I traversed left to the start of the Merkl Couloir and looked up, craning my neck. The gully above was like a big chasm. It was very steep and seamed with rock steps but it would go. And the rock steps – could they be climbed free? They were heavily featured, so they were sure to be climbable without recourse to artificial means, and higher up the gully flattened out.

Menwhile, the sun had come out and the snow was getting soft, making every movement strenuous and energy-sapping, even when climbing back down. Everything we did was a torment.

Just before midday we arrived back at Camp 4. Hans, Gert and Werner had been there again. They had ferried heavy loads up from Camp 3 – ropes, provisions and tents – an incredible achievement considering the height gain and the difficulty of the climbing. The post had arrived, too, with letters for us. But first, there were other things to occupy us.

Far below we could see two figures climbing, slogging up towards the Merkl Icefield, moving very slowly and sinking deep into the soft snow of the trail but not giving up despite the terrible heat. They were carrying huge rucksacks. It was Hermann and Gerhard. The expressions on their faces betrayed the effort of will required to get to Camp 4.

Hermann descended again immediately while Gerhard pitched his tent. He was staying with us at Camp 4.

Now everything was in place, the set-up perfect for the summit push. All the camps were occupied and everyone knew what needed to be done. All the team wanted to do their best to ensure that the climb was now brought to a successful conclusion. Even little Peter, who had been ill for so long, was back up on the face helping out. However, the team did not have unlimited energy reserves and it was now or never. Any hesistation now would spell failure.

We had no way of knowing whether the people down at Base Camp realized just how close we were to the summit. Their life down there was very different to ours, but they, too, were keeping busy. They radioed in three times a day and during one of the calls Michl, the climbing leader, let us know that they were not just sitting around playing cards down there.

There were now three tents pitched on a narrow shelf of ice in the bergschrund of the Merkl Icefield: one for Gerhard, one for Peter and Felix and one for Günther and I. Herrligkoffer said he was with us in spirit. He seemed eager for the summit assault to begin – or did he have a new plan up his sleeve?

Hans and Gert came up again with more loads but left again immediately. No one wanted to descend in the midday heat.

It was still early when we crawled into our sleeping bags. Peter and Felix wanted to take a tent up to Camp 5 early next day and pitch it there if possible.

Herrligkoffer: 'On 26 June Felix Kuen and Peter Scholz set off to establish Camp 5 at the end of the Merkl Icefield. They got up at 2:15 a.m. and went out into the cold night to try and follow the trail made by the Messner brothers the previous day, but the tracks had been obliterated by the wind. In their rucksacks they carried tents and 200m of line with which to establish Camp 5, the assault camp.'

All the preparations had now been made and the load supply system organized. Although petty rivalries still existed within the team everyone without exception was now working towards the common goal. Karl, meanwhile, was obviously keeping all his options open for the final summit push.

After just four hours Felix and Peter reached the spot beneath the vertical summit headwall that had been earmarked for the assault camp. They pitched the little tent on the narrow ice ledge that they had widened and flattened out.

Herrligkoffer: 'They used their axes to chop out a flat ledge on the 50 degree ice slope below a rock spur near the entrance to the Merkl Couloir. It was very strenuous work but by 11:30 they had managed it. A little red Klepper tent at 7350m formed the last place of refuge before the summit – it was more of a bivouac than a camp.'

When Felix and Peter returned they were happy with their efforts and very thirsty too. Although pleased with our words of praise they were not at all happy with the weather and the banks of cloud rolling in to the south. Were we about to have another break in the weather?

Kuen: 'We are now pressed for time! After various changes, and taking into account the physical performance and the general condition of each individual team member, the following plan has now been finalized: Reinhold Messner, Peter Scholz and I will climb the last quarter of the Rupal Face as a rope of three, ascending by way of the Merkl Couloir and the South Shoulder to the Summit. Since there is only room for three men in the tent at Camp 5, Reinhold, Günther and Gerd Baur will fix around 200m of rope in the Couloir before the summit push.'

It was only later – years later – that I learned about these logistics. And I had no idea where Felix had got this plan from. We never spoke about it. However, the ropes had already been dumped at Camp 5.

Kuen: 'After we set off, a team comprising Mändl, Saler, Haim, Baur and Günther will have the task of fixing a further 300m of rope in the Merkl Couloir and then waiting at Camp 5 or Camp 4 until we return.'

No one apart from us new anything about the plan, and Felix never mentioned the logistics. He also said nothing about the fact that, if the weather was good, a further rope consisting of those men from the two higher camps who felt fit enough would be freed up to repeat the summit assault.

Was it simply that the climbers at Camp 4 were talking at cross purposes? Each man had his own very different thoughts about the summit, but no one talked about it. It was a bit like the Tower of Babel up there, a place where misunderstanding and confusion were rife. Maybe it was the altitude.

It was 26 June 1970. Who was responsible for the planning? Certainly not Felix, at least not he alone. Peter had no particular ambitions. The summit was, after all, a collective goal and not an egotistical objective. Perhaps there had been some kind of secret agreement made between Karl and Felix; new plans that we knew nothing about. For my part, I knew of no plan. Down at Base Camp I had not been privy to Herrligkoffer's rules and regulations, the documentation and the rite of hoisting up the flag on the summit. Günther and I had climbed the route up to the final camp full of trust in our own abilities and in the solidarity shown by our leader. Naturally we were also ambitious and our eyes were wide open, but we were also open to any reasonable suggestions. The route to the summit was now open – but the question of who and when and how remained.

Even months after the expedition I did not suspect that any secret deals had been struck. Naive as I was, I believed in the process of natural selection whereby the best would be given their chance.

Chapter X

The Decision

The upper part of the Rupal Face. Camp 4 is between the lower seracs. The Merkl Icefield lies in shadow. Above it is the Merkl Couloir.

At this point in time the difficulties in the Merkl Couloir are an unknown quantity; no one knows for sure whether it can be climbed in its entirety.

Felix Kuen

Camp 4. Scholz and Kuen in the foreground.

On Friday 26 June Reinhold Messner held a radio conversation with Dr Herrligkoffer from Camp 4. Messner expressed his concern about the cloud formation and asked for a weather report. This was not yet available but it was agreed that the report would be communicated to the Messner brothers, who were soon to transfer up to Camp 5, later that evening using a system of coloured signal flares: red = bad weather, blue = good weather, red and blue = questionable weather. This arrangement was made because there was no radio signal between Camp 5 and Base Camp.

Felix Kuen

That evening a red rocket was mistakenly fired from Base Camp despite the good weather report.

Felix Kuen

Reinhold must thus have assumed that the weather report was bad.

Felix Kuen

The Red Rocket

By the end of June all the preparations for the first summit assault had been made. The supply line was functioning well and down at Base Camp everyone was hoping that there would be no further delays. Losing time now would mean losing any chance of the summit.

We five were now so high up on the face that I felt very remote and exposed out there on the Merkl Icefield; it was like being lost in space. Günther and I were now constantly looking up. If the weather stayed as it was there could be no hesitation, we told ourselves. Herrligkoffer's first 'plan of attack' was now two weeks out of date but there was no second plan. What should we do if it started snowing again in two days' time?

Gerhard sat on his air bed outside the tent, Felix and Peter were cooking, Günther was in the tent. He blinked as he stepped out, the sunlight was so dazzling. I held the Teleport apparatus, a heavy-duty radio weighing several kilogrammes, in my right hand and pressed the 'speak' button. I was talking on the radio to Base Camp for the last time. On this day, the 26th of June, shortly before 2 o'clock in the afternoon, the decision was made.

'This is Camp 4. Base Camp please copy.'

'Karl here, Base Camp. How are you?'

We talked for a long time; about equipment that needed to be brought up; about oxygen bottles and provisions; about the forthcoming summit push and the allocation of various tasks. Then the conversation turned to the weather.

'There's a wide bank of cloud in the west and east. The clouds are getting nearer every hour. We'll have to hurry,' I said.

185

'It won't hold much longer,' Karl replied.

'Günther, Gerhard and I are going up to Camp 5 today. We are going to set off from here when the sun has disappeared behind the West Col. About five o'clock or thereabouts.'

Later, Herrligkoffer had this to say: 'In the afternoon of 26 June Reinhold Messner made radio contact from Camp 4. He said that he, his brother and Gerd Baur were going up to Camp 5 that evening. Felix Kuen and Peter Scholz had established the camp that morning. He talked about a wide bank of cloud coming in from the south and the need to make a quick decision.'

Impressed by Herrligkoffer's attentiveness, I dared to make the following suggestion:

'If the weather report is good we will fix the Merkl Couloir tomorrow, as far up as we can. If the weather report is bad I want to try to go up on my own, as far as I can – maybe even to the summit. Otherwise, if the weather turns bad we won't have a chance. Preparing the route up the Merkl Couloir in stages would be impossible then.'

Karl was enthusiastic about my suggestion. Even he knew that if the weather took a turn for the worse only a lightning fast push would stand any chance of success. Felix Kuen, who was listening in full of scepticism, obviously thought otherwise. But he said nothing.

Was there some kind of unspoken agreement between him and Herrligkoffer? What did I know. It was then that I had the idea with the rockets.

'Karl', I said, 'can you use the rockets to give us the weather report at eight this evening? Red for bad weather, green for good weather. We won't have a radio at Camp 5; it's too heavy.'

'Good idea, but we've only got red and blue rockets', said Karl after a while.

No problem, I thought.

'Right then, we'll do it like this: red means bad weather and I'll try it alone. I'll go up as far as I can and make sure I'm back at Camp 5 by evening. Blue means the weather

Hans Saler operating the heavy radio set.

report is good. Three of us will fix the lower part of the Merkl Couloir and over the next few days we'll go for the summit as a rope of four. If the weather report is doubtful, shoot off one blue and one red and we'll decide up here what we're going to do. It all depends.'

The colours of the rockets and their meanings were repeated several times. There was no doubt in my mind about our arrangement.

187

Without saying much the three of us – Gerhard, Günther and I – got ready for the climb. The sun had by now disappeared behind the West Col. The rucksacks were lying ready. It was time to go.

Odd patches of mist grew like mushrooms out of the uniform sea of cloud to the south. The formations changed shape; one looked like a hammer, another like the head of an animal. Günther coughed. His coughing was nothing to do with a cold. He was saying we had to go.

The three of us set off up the Merkl Icefield. At about eight o'clock in the evening we stopped for a few minutes. It was already dark. We stared expectantly in the direction of Base Camp and waited for the agreed signal.

At eight o'clock on the dot, a red rocket went up. It was far below in the valley but clearly recognizable – a red rocket. And only one. We waited for a second, but there was none.

So the weather report was bad, we thought. We were disappointed, but the decision was an easy one. It was up to us what we did next. I did not hesitate for long, a few minutes, maybe and then, for me, it was clear: we get there before the bad weather. I would attempt the summit climb tomorrow, alone and moving as fast as possible. That is what I had agreed with Karl.

We carried on climbing and not long afterwards crawled into the little assault tent beneath the Merkl Couloir. It was a spartan camp, much too cramped for three men, and the ground was hard. Ice had formed on the flysheet.

'I'll go as far as I can tomorrow', I said, 'and you two fix the lowest section of the Couloir.'

'There's only 200m of rope, though, Reinhold.'

'Chop it into pieces and use it on the hardest sections,' I said.

Conversation was reduced to the bare necessities. Excitement ran high. There was a strange quiet inside the tent. Günther and I lay next to each other. Gerhard lay across the foot end. It was cold, dry and very cramped. We dozed a little, but no one could sleep in that situation. It was going to be a miserable night. With no sleeping bags or stove there was no way we could recover from the climbing. And it was getting colder and colder, maybe 30°C below zero. There was nothing to drink, so we were constantly thirsty. The feeling of absolute remoteness remained, even when I nodded off briefly, and every time I woke up it was like looking into a bottomless pit as that huge great wave of a wall sucked at our little tent. Lying there 4000m above Base Camp, it was like I was floating – somewhere between Heaven and Earth. Above us was the Merkl Couloir, the crux that no one knew. Somewhere far above was the summit. No, there could be no worse place on Earth than here. This emptiness – just what were we doing here?

The Key to the Summit

At two o'clock in the morning I was still crouching in the tent. I had not heard the alarm I had set for midnight. I was still dressed: three layers of legwear and five layers on my upper body, none of which I had taken off in the tent. All I needed now were my overtrousers, my boots and my anorak, the pockets of which held the essential items I needed for my summit bid: a photo of the face and a Minox camera. My movements were well practised yet somehow clumsy and slow.

It was still night. A feeble light filtered through the walls of the little assault tent as I put on my headtorch. I knew the tent was pitched on a vertical mountain wall of rock and ice with nothing but the bottomless void below. I knew all this without looking out of the tent. Above was only the sky, and the sky was clear and starry – a lucky break.

I sat on a half-inflated camping mat and finished getting dressed. Günther and Gerhard seemed to be sleeping still. I took my crampons, ice axe and overgloves. Finally I stuffed the headtorch battery into the chest pocket of my anorak and crawled out of the tent. At first I felt small and insignificant, a little lost. Our campsite was narrow and cramped and still in shadow but high up in the deepest recesses of the Merkl Couloir the moon shone brightly, so that was what I headed for – onwards and upwards!

That first look up caused a shudder to run down my spine. This was going to be the hardest climb of my life, I thought. As if on a second level of consciousness, I watched myself climbing the Couloir. Alone on this seemingly endless 5000m sweep of face, suddenly it was only the detail that was important.

Rivulets of fine powder snow sloughed off down onto the sugared slopes beneath my feet as I climbed the first rock rib. Then I arrived at the first steep step. Carefully removing two pairs of gloves, I stuffed them in the pockets of my anorak and started climbing, the front points of one crampon biting on a tiny edge, one white gloved hand pressed flat against the rock. The ice axe dangled from my wrist and made a bright ringing sound as the metal bounced against rock, making strange sounds in the night.

I had taken silk gloves with me for hard sections of climbing like this one and I felt safe wearing them even on hard rock pitches. A deep feeling of calm had come over me and at first I did not even notice how thin the air was. Common sense told me not to think, just to keep on climbing. It was that second level of consciousness thing again.

I was soon standing beneath another steep section. It looked difficult, more difficult than it really was, probably about grade IV – hard enough, but still okay to solo. I was still climbing steadily and fast. I was confident that I would soon be half way up the Merkl Couloir, but still I did not look down. There was no point. Since finding my rhythm I was climbing like I always did, totally focused and at one with myself. The route was clear and looked as if it would go, so on I went, keeping moving, keeping warm, feeling quite safe.

190

There was now a little more moonlight and my own shadow kept pace with me as I climbed up a steep snow slope. I did not rest much; I just kept on climbing, heading straight up. Again I found myself standing beneath an overhanging chockstone. The bed of the gully was plastered in ice and the exit further up at the end of the blockage full of powder snow. At this altitude and with the clumsy, heavy boots I was wearing, such a steep pitch was clearly too dangerous, maybe even impossible. At any rate, I would not be able to down-climb it. I had gone too high. So back I went, looking for an exit lower down. The gully closed in on me like a chimney.

I had decided to descend a little way and try my luck out to the right, hoping that the right-hand containing wall of the gully would offer a feasible continuation route, but it was not to be. I was about to give up and go back down to Camp 5 when another possibility presented itself, a last chance, in the shape of a sloping ramp leading up and right. It seemed to offer the only possibility, my last chance if you like. The climbing was easier than I had thought – grade III perhaps – and the rock was only partly verglassed. Only the flatter holds were full of snow and the ramp was long enough at two pitches not to be missed on the way back down. This was it: the key to avoid the difficult steep section in the Merkl Couloir. Suddenly I felt safe again and every bit as sure of myself as I would have felt on a route in the Alps.

Two Worlds – One Goal

Herrligkoffer: 'On 27 June at about 6:10 in the morning I saw a dark object moving quickly up the ice about half way up the Merkl Couloir. After twenty minutes it disappeared again from view.'

The South Spur at nearly 8000m.

I must now be at about 7800m, I thought. To the left, high above me, I could just make out a notch on the skyline – the end of the Merkl Couloir? I would soon be out of the gully then. There was just one last steep section to do before I reached the ramp that led across below the South Shoulder to the South-East Ridge.

Nothing could stop me now, even though I was quite alone and climbing on top of the world. I had certainly never known exposure like it. A fleeting glance down was enough, as the face became lost in the shadowy depths of the valley below. But when I looked up into the bright morning light it was into a different, alien world. There were now only about 300m of vertical height between me and the summit, I reckoned. It was nothing compared to the 4200m that lay below. My hopes grew and with them my confidence. I thought of this last section, the summit structure of Nanga Parbat, as a mountain in itself – a floating mountain, an island above the clouds.

Günther's Decision

It was getting warm now, hot even, and the heat from the sun was taking more out of me than the thin air.

I climbed up and right across the ramp. It was hard breaking trail – it had been hard for hours! I was nowhere near as fast as I had been that morning. The route finding was tough, but it was the sun that really drained me. The temperature was way below zero but the sun's rays burned as if through a magnifying glass. Again and again I stopped and rested, ramming my ice axe into the snow and leaning hard on it, often looking down to make sure I had memorized the route for my descent. Suddenly I stopped short. Was that someone following me up? There, a short way below, was a climber. Who could it be? It was Günther, no doubt about it! He was climbing fast and well, as if he were trying to make up time. I looked down again and watched him, a little irritated, then decided to wait. The next thing I knew, Günther was standing beside me, breathing hard.

'How did you find the route?' I asked.

'Your tracks. The route is logical anyway.'

'And what about the bit where the gully closes up?'

'Up the ramp. No other possibility.'

'Were you roped up?'

'Only to begin with.'

We did not talk much. Günther had climbed the whole of the Merkl Couloir in less than four hours – almost 600m of vertical height, at this altitude! There was no longer any question: we would carry on together. We belonged together and we would soon be on the summit, I thought.

'And where is Gerhard?' I asked.

'Gone back down. He's got a sore throat.'

We started along the big traverse leading out right beneath the South Shoulder to the South-East Ridge, climbing one behind the other.

It was now late morning. We climbed slowly, one breaking trail out front while the other rested. We stopped frequently, just to get our breath. The rest breaks got longer, partly because of the heat and partly because we had to keep searching for the best route. All we really wanted to do was give in to the compulsion to rest, but the thought of going back down never crossed our minds.

Our mountain was now hidden in cloud but the sun shone through at frequent intervals. The mist played around us and below us. Now and then, when the clouds parted, we could see right down to the dark Rupal Valley but we could not make out Base Camp – it was much too far away. The people down at Base couldn't see us either, I thought.

Moving at a snail's pace now, we traversed across the snow and ice slopes beneath the South Shoulder. A little way below us, the Rupal Face dropped sheer to the valley. But even though this mountain face is unique on Earth, we no longer noticed it. We just kept climbing – onwards and upwards! As each hour passed, we got a tiny bit higher. The snow was deep and soft. The sun burned down on our backs

The upper half of the Rupal Face. The last traverse crosses the snowfield at the top right of the picture.

and reflected back off the snow, the rays deflected through the mist at right angles onto the face.

The sun was our worst enemy now, it made us tired, apathetic, sleepy. And the heat! During our rest breaks we crumpled up on the snow, the altitude now just a secondary cause of our lethargy, but there was nowhere to crawl away and hide – nowhere. Now and again, one of us would mumble a word of encouragement and carry on climbing. We understood each other so well, even without words. The other would then drag himself upright and take a few more stumbling steps up. I would manage just two steps before leaning over my axe for a rest, lungs rasping.

We traversed to the right, gaining height all the while, then trudged up a last steep snow slope, heading straight for a dip in the ridge. Günther took photographs; I snapped a few too. That is how I got that last picture of Günther. It shows him on the last few metres of the route, topping out on the highest rock and ice wall in the world.

Up on the ridge, Günther stopped and waved excitedly, then shouted. What was he trying to say? That he could see the summit, that we would soon be there. I could not understand the words but still I knew what he meant.

I followed in Günther's tracks and soon joined him on the crest of the ridge. As we stood there between two worlds, finally we knew that we could reach the summit. Between reason and emotion there was no more room for any other considerations. Below us was the Rupal Flank; ahead, barely 100m away – the summit!

All we now had to do was get there. There was no room for emotion, for fear, no yesterday and no tomorrow – just the summit and the two of us. My first impressions on emerging onto the ridge from the South Face was for me the most powerful moment of the entire Nanga Parbat Expedition. Everything seemed so unreal, so quiet. And there was Günther, right next to me.

196

Günther Messner below the summit ridge.

To the right, beneath the ridge, we could see the Silver Plateau and the Silver Saddle. They looked close enough to touch. And there, too, was Rakhiot Peak. Below us, in the South-East corrie, the blanket of cloud swirled and shifted. I thought of Buhl, going over his climb in my head, following his tracks in my mind's eye to the top and back again. My thoughts turned, too, to Aschenbrenner and Schneider, to the brilliant Tyrolean high-altitude mountaineer Erwin Schneider, to Rebitsch and many more, and to the expedition leaders, who had never made it up so high. Günther and I talked briefly about Merkl and Welzenbach. It was as if they were there with us.

Ahead was the steep sweep of ridge leading to the highest point. The summit was nothing more than a modest pyramid of snow. To the left was the South Shoulder, a snow-covered spur of rock. Whenever the tatters of mist blew past it looked further away than it was.

Slowly but steadily we climbed higher, wading through powder snow and then crunching along on the hard, wind-

197

View from the summit to the south with the South Shoulder visible on the right.

blown crest of the ridge. The terrain was now flat, and devoid of any technical difficulties. The snow was dazzling and everything seemed smooth and flat but the snow slope underfoot was rough and pitted with holes that we kept stumbling into blindly, confused by the diffuse light and the mist. A little unsure of myself now, I prodded the snow in front of me with my axe or my boot, step by step, feeling for firm ground beneath.

Günther and I were now standing next to each other on a little patch of snow, chatting away as the clouds swirled around the summit, and watching the magical display of wind-blown snow crystals and spindrift being whipped across the ridge. Or was it the spirits of the high mountains carrying all before them? Günther stood there, the shaft of his axe buried in the snow, fiddling with his camera while I climbed on over the South Shoulder. Plumes of spindrift swept over the wind-sculpted channels in the snow before me. The wind whistled. Günther clicked the shutter, folded

198

the camera away, pulled his gloves from his pocket and brushed the buried ice axe with his fist. Luckily it did not fall over. Awkwardly, he pulled his gloves on again. They were plastered in snow, stiff with ice. Then, taking the axe in his right hand, he moved off again, the camera dangling from his chest, the wind blowing loose snow from the soles of his boots with every step he took.

For me, the most important thing now was to keep moving, so I did not allow myself any further distractions and only stopped to rest and look around again once I had reached the col between the South Summit and the Main Summit.

Günther was stopping more and more frequently to rest and take photographs. He had a big, large-format camera and several rolls of colour film.

I focused my eyes on the last sharp peak, the summit ridge dead ahead, with only the sky above. Just a few minutes more, I thought. The last section of the ridge looked so short, but I had actually been climbing for a good half hour or more since leaving the col. Time and space have no real meaning at such altitudes. Here, nothing is the same; none of the usual rules apply. We drift along, floating high above the valleys, yet feel so heavy. So far away from the world, and so far away from ourselves.

The Summit

Suddenly I found myself standing on a final dome of firn snow – the summit of Nanga Parbat. I had a quick look around but it was nothing like the fairy-tale world I had imagined. I was exhausted and there was not much to see. I stood there and did not really understand why. The realization dawned in slow motion: this was it, a moment of suspended animation to mark the end of our slow progress.

Günther sat further down and took photographs. Then he followed me up, step by step, and joined me on the top. He took his mittens off and extended a hand towards me. Two cold hands clasped in a brief embrace. Because we were there together there was a feeling of satisfaction, a kind of happiness, despite the tiredness and lethargy.

The fact that Günther was there with me makes that hour on the summit so valuable to me, even now. The memory of it is still good, despite the run of the mill daily routines of the intervening years. I can still see his eyes, as clearly as I could then. We had both taken off our snow goggles – I have no idea why. At the time, neither of us thought about snow blindness.

Since we had never been on the top of an 8000m mountain before we did what we had done a thousand times before when topping out on a climb: we shook hands, rested and looked at the view. I was surprised when Günther clapped me on the shoulder. Maybe I should have said something, but at that moment I did not know what to say.

We took some photographs of each other and had a good look around. We now needed to make our descent. We had maybe an hour of daylight left. It was late, maybe too late.

As we were getting ready to go I tried to pull my big, thick Norwegian mittens on again but they were frozen stiff and I could not get them on over the other gloves. I had a reserve pair, though, so I just dumped the two useless lumps of felt, ice and snow on the first rocks to the west of the summit dome and piled a few stones on top. It was a marker of sorts, a sign that we had been there. Perhaps that little cairn on the summit of Nanga Parbat was a kind of symbol – but of what, we did not know. Günther smiled at my indulgence. A cairn – what for? The wind would soon demolish it, just as it had erased any trace of Buhl's ascent. We looked back one last time and then, slowly, we started down.

At the time I had no idea that my mittens would later provide the proof that we had indeed been to the summit. I only knew that some people needed proof of everything. Felix and Peter found my gloves a day later – they must have thought they were just a couple of pieces of frozen felt – but could not identify them as definitely being mine. Later there were people who used that – and the fact that all of our summit photos were lost – to cast doubts on our summit claim. If I were to say to those people now that the proof that we made it to the summit lies in the fact that we shook hands, smiled and clapped each other on the shoulder, and that we looked back one last time during our descent, they would probably still shrug their shoulders and demand photographic evidence.

The Descent Begins

Slowly, we began our descent. To the west was a bank of cloud; above, the sky glowed red. Günther followed me as best he could. Fresh snow and spindrift lay in our tracks. Günther was lagging further behind. It was now clear to me that Günther was very tired. He had been following me all day long and had over exerted himself. Perhaps he was suffering from altitude sickness. He had climbed the Merkl Couloir in less than four hours and the effort was now making itself felt, I thought, but I still couldn't imagine that he would collapse on me now.

I stopped and waited at the col between the South Shoulder and the ridge. Günther arrived and pointed with his axe to the right. It looked like he wanted to descend to the west. At first, I did not understand what he was suggesting. Down the Diamir Face? I waved back, dismissing the idea out of hand. 'No, we can't do that,' I said.

'It's easier,' he countered.

'We have to go down the way we came,' I said, trying hard to hide my concerns.

'Too difficult,' said Günther.

'But we came up the Merkl Couloir.'

'I'm so tired.'

'We'll be even more tired tomorrow. We have to lose some height before it gets dark.'

'But not the way we came up. We have to find an easier route.'

I did not insist. Perhaps I should have done.

It would have been so easy just to stay where we were but I did not want to do that and neither did Günther. He was not expecting help to arrive the next day, otherwise we could have simply waited.

It was then that I remembered the red rocket. The bad weather would be coming in soon. We needed to get out of there, fast. I knew only that we had to get down, somewhere. Where could we bivouac, I asked myself, and where could we be seen from the Merkl Couloir? Günther still wanted to drop down to the right of the ridge.

'It's not easy down to the west, either,' I said.

'But easier.'

'And tomorrow?'

'Maybe we could traverse back into the Couloir lower down, at the Merkl Gap. Otherwise we'll have to shout for a rope. The others will fix the Couloir.'

We did not have a rope, since we had both set off soloing from Camp 5. It was looking bad.

I took out a tattered and creased colour photograph of the Rupal Flank that I had stuck in my pocket as an emergency route-finding aid. From the picture it looked possible to traverse into the Merkl Couloir from the Merkl Gap – theoretically, at least. Down to the Gap, then, I thought, and set off. At the time I had no way of knowing what the consequences of this action might be but at least we were losing height, and by the only means possible. In Günther's

The summit region. This photograph was the only visual aid to orientation that Reinhold Messner had with him.

state it would have been too dangerous to descend the Rupal Face and it would soon be dark, so we were forced to piece together an alternative plan. There was nothing else for it but to descend the easier Diamir side to the Gap at the upper end of the Merkl Couloir, I thought. I am not saying that there was no other route, but right then, the west-side descent suddenly became the obvious one for us to go for. A third alternative did not even feature in our discussions and at 8000m you can not afford to start searching around for the best way down. The decision was made; we would descend the Diamir Face. It was now just a question of survival. Our odyssey on Nanga Parbat had begun.

It was to end tragically but this does not mean that our decision to descend into the unknown was an unreasonable one to make. In the circumstances it was the only possible way out of the very serious situation we were in.

We climbed down a diagonal ramp. It was slow work. We traversed across snow gullies and steep rock steps, climbing mostly on all fours, faces to the wall, before standing upright again and facing out, down to the valley.

After more than an hour of this, we reached a flat hollow of snow at the foot of the craggy summit structure. We had gone wrong, too low, and were a good way to the west and below the Merkl Gap. So back we went, trudging our way up another snow slope. I took the lead and went looking for a place to bivi up on the Gap.

Günther followed, very slowly, every step requiring a big effort. The terrain was not steep – like a ski slope, maybe – but he still kept stopping to rest. Then he would take another step. On it went.

We had been up in the Death Zone for hours now, walking the fine line between survival and dying. We were not really conscious of being in a life-threatening situation, however. Although we were dreadfully tired, parched, hungry and a little desperate by now, we could still hope that somehow we would get through it. I knew that we still had the hardest part of the descent to do, whichever way we went, but my main concern was now for Günther. Would he survive the night at this altitude with no shelter and exposed to the cold? Help was a long way off. It felt like we were on another planet.

Bivouac

I eventually found a hollow with overhanging crags above that would make a good place for a bivi and scraped the snow to one side with the edge of my boot. I knelt down and fiddled about with my crampon straps. Trying to loosen them with stiff, frozen fingers was a real nuisance. Günther arrived and I showed him the facilities: a bank of snow to crouch on. We took off our boots, wrapped our feet in a section of space blanket – a thin, aluminium-coated laminate designed to reflect back the body's own heat – stuck our feet back inside our two pairs of inner boots and sat on the outers, using them as an insulating layer between our backsides and the ground. Then we waited, apathetic yet strangely alert to the possibility that something unexpected might happen.

The temperature could no longer be measured in terms of degrees minus – maybe 30 or 40 – it was simply deadly cold. We constantly reminded each other to keep wiggling our toes but soon we were totally chilled to the bone and shivering uncontrollably. Our situation had something of the surreal, something spooky about it as we slipped into a semiconscious state of waiting. We wrapped more of the foil around us and sat there apathetically, hunched over, for hours; three, four, maybe five hours – I do not know. Like zombies. Wretched and freezing to death, as the wind howled and the storm blew in.

'Reinhold, give me the blanket,' my brother pleaded.

'What blanket?'

'The one on the ground there.'

'There's no blanket.'

Günther was hallucinating.

'Give me the blanket,' he repeated and reached out to grab something.

'You're crazy. There is no blanket.'

'What?' Günther snatched at the ground again.

'I'll explain it all to you later,' I said. 'Can you still feel your toes?'

'Don't know.'

'You must keep them moving.'

It was very cold: −30°C, maybe more, with an icy wind. The cold penetrated every fibre of the body like an indiscriminate pain. The wind blew in gusts, whistling around the rocks. You could hear the wind-blown snow as it flew around the edges of the rocks, and the cracking of the ice. There were stars now, too, shining with a harsh bright light. It was like being somewhere in outer space.

We huddled closer together. We had wrapped the space blanket so tightly around us that the wind could not get hold of it but our heads were free, covered only by our caps, which offered precious little protection. We just sat there and waited; waited for morning. We did nothing else. We no longer spoke or made plans, keeping thought to a minimum. When it is that cold, you can not think anyway. There was one thing I knew, though: you get warmer when you die.

It was now about −40°C, although the exact temperature was immaterial. As long as we could still summon some energy to combat the cold we would stay alive. It was a murderously cold night and we getting confused and desperate. For those who have not experienced climbing in the Death Zone, the cold up there is much worse than on the Matterhorn, for example, because the air is so thin and the wind makes everything much worse. And there was nothing

The Diamir Face. The bivouac was in the second notch to the right of the summit.

we could do about it. We kept moving our toes but we could no longer feel them. All we felt were pain and fear.

It was not yet daylight but it was light enough to see. Günther suddenly stood up and walked away. What was wrong with him? Where was he going? He stamped around in a circle, moaning to himself. Although he said nothing, Günther's condition was worrying me, so at about six o'clock in the morning I started shouting for help, hoping to establish contact with the others. Perhaps there was still someone at Camp 5, I thought. From the notch to the east of the bivi site I could see down to the Merkl Couloir. A steep wall plastered in snow dropped away beneath my feet. The view down was terrifying.

When I got back to the bivi I tried to appear confident and give the impression that there might still be some hope. With a calmness that surprised even me, I tried to console Günther, but I knew full well that without help we were lost.

I traversed back again a little way towards the Merkl Couloir, about 50m away from the bivi site, and looked down into the void. A hundred metres further down I could make out our tracks from yesterday but it would have been impossible – or at the very least, extremely difficult – to reach them from where I was standing. Without a rope it was unthinkable. Snow was plastered all over loose rock and below me the terrain was plumb vertical. In Günther's critical condition it would be too dangerous to attempt it. I grabbed hold of a lump of rock with one hand, peered down and shouted for help. There was no answer, just the wind and that awful silence. I was getting hoarse, almost choking, and a feeling of helplessness engulfed me as I felt my reserves of strength and my hope fading. I had to keep this from Günther. He was hallucinating, his movements were even slower than mine and he was acting irrationally. He was having to stop and rest after every step now.

I realized with a mixture of curiousity and shock that I was also losing the ability to reason properly, too.

Our state of mind was similar to that of a patient coming round after a general anaesthetic. Himalayan literature is full of reports about strange behaviour caused by lack of oxygen and exhaustion, but it was too late to do anything about it. The only solution was to lose height.

No Rescue

I went over to the rocks again and looked down. Holding tight with one hand, I leaned further out and shouted repeatedly down into the Merkl Couloir.

'Help! We need a rope!'

I continued shouting for about two hours in all, but in vain. There was no one to be seen. I took a break and walked back over to Günther.

'They must have heard me,' I said.

'In this wind?' Günther replied.

There wasn't much more to say, so I went back to where I could see down onto the Rupal Face and suddenly there was someone there! Far below in the Merkl Couloir I could just make out two tiny figures. There was no doubt about it – they were getting nearer, climbing up towards us. They are looking for us, I thought, and shouted again but no one answered. But the two tiny figures were still climbing.

'Help!' I shouted again.

I went back to Günther, by now convinced that they were on their way up to help us.

'Günther, they're coming!'

'Where?'

'Middle of the Merkl Couloir.'

'Who?'

'Don't know.'

'How many of them?'

'Two.'

'At last!'

Günther got to his feet again, moving slowly and unsteadily and swaying alarmingly.

Back at my viewpoint, I could now recognize the two climbers. It was Felix and Peter. Peter was standing beneath the last rock pitch in the couloir, belaying around his axe. Felix was leading; I could tell it was him by the way he moved.

'Hello!' I shouted again, 'Give us a rope!'

Felix stopped and looked up at me. They must have heard our shouts for help, otherwise they would not have come, I thought. Still convinced that they were only there on our account, I signalled that we were descending. 'Were you on the summit?' were the only words from Felix that I could understand clearly. The wind meant it was hard to make ourselves understood.

'Yes!' I screamed.

We continued shouting backwards and forwards but I could not understand everything. It was stormy at the notch.

Felix carried on climbing, following the clearly defined tracks we had made yesterday. He was moving up towards the notch where I was waiting for him. He was coming closer but there was still 80 to 100m between us. I could not climb down to meet him but maybe I could pull his rope up to me, I thought.

Perched on my narrow ledge, I clumsily joined several pieces of thin accessory cord together that I had in my pocket. Five or six metres in all – too short! The cord, which I carried for emergencies, was far too short to pull up Felix's rope, but how else could I belay him up the last few metres of the pitch? The last section was vertical and looked extremely hard. In fact, from my position at the notch, it looked unclimbable, but since climbs usually look easier from below I decided to wait and see what happened.

Suddenly Felix started traversing further right. It looked as if he had changed his mind. Perhaps the wall pitch really was too steep. It was only now that it became clear to me that Felix was going for the summit. This was something I had not anticipated and for a moment I was stunned into inactivity. What were we to do without a rope? I had to change strategies – and fast.

'Hello', I shouted again. And again.

Felix kept stopping and looking up at me. How could I

tempt him up here? Or was he still looking for an alternative route? If only we could make ourselves understood better.

'You can go to the summit from where we are', I tried to explain. 'The direct route – left round the South Shoulder – the way we came down.' 'It's faster,' I added. Felix seemed to have understood, yet he kept climbing.

It later transpired that Felix Kuen had misunderstood my shouts. He had indeed taken a more direct route to the summit, going left around the South Shoulder, but not via the notch where I had been standing.

My efforts had all been in vain. Neither my request that Felix and Peter climb up to us nor the promise of a faster, more direct route to the summit had worked; we still had not managed to get the rope. We would only have needed it to descend the Merkl Couloir – just one abseil would have done it. Felix and Peter could have gone to the summit from here, I thought. We were now in a desperate situation. I had to try and stay calm.

It was not just that we had been physically too far apart that had made it impossible to communicate but also the fact that neither of us was in full command of his faculties.

Kuen: 'I saw a figure above me, bobbing about intermittently on the ridge between the Merkl Gap and the South Summit. He was waving and seemed to be shouting. I didn't understand anything as the wind was blowing too hard over the ridge, or maybe the blood was pounding too hard in my ears.'

At the time, it slowly became clear to me that Felix and Peter were acting on instructions but surely they must have seen that Günther and I were trapped. *Felix reckoned that the only thing he understood was that 'Is everything okay?'* Without a rope we were lost, but otherwise, yes, everything was okay.

Kuen: 'When I got to within 100m or so of the figure on the ridge I recognized it as Reinhold Messner and stopped. Peter Scholz, belayed below me, was doing another repair job on his crampons.'

I understood his question to be 'Are you both okay?' and answered in the affirmative.

'Yes! Everything's okay, Felix,' I shouted, as if to reassure both of us. After all, in the Death Zone, 'okay' and 'fit and well' is a relative concept.

Kuen: 'I was feeling weak and close to collapse but we were within sight of the summit and I did not want to give up, so I took a Pervitin tablet and soon felt fit again.'

Yes, we were okay. I had been shouting for help for three hours because we needed a rope, but otherwise everything was okay. Maybe I even said 'otherwise' – 'otherwise everything is okay' – but I can not be sure. It was certainly meant that way.

I was so sure that the two of them were coming up with the sole intention of helping us that I debated how best to top rope them up to me, hence the accessory cord and the 'okay'. But the terrain really was too steep. And then it dawned on me that they were intending to go for the summit, just like we had discussed the day before.

How were we going to get down now? For a moment I was paralysed by bewilderment. I knew that the others could only help us now on their way down.

No, no, the wall pitch must be impossible from below, I now told myself. I could not see down it exactly but Felix and Peter had taken a detour so it must have been too risky even for good climbers like Felix and Peter. Nothing untoward must be allowed to happen now, or else we would all be lost – all four of us.

Kuen: 'From where I was standing it would have been impossible to bridge the distance between us. The ridge above was heavily corniced. To attempt such a pitch at 7900m would have been suicidal. If you fell off there you would go 1000m with no way of stopping yourself.'

Felix carried on climbing and at first I couldn't understand it. He must have misunderstood me, I thought. Either that or the altitude has made him confused. Peter seemed totally apathetic.

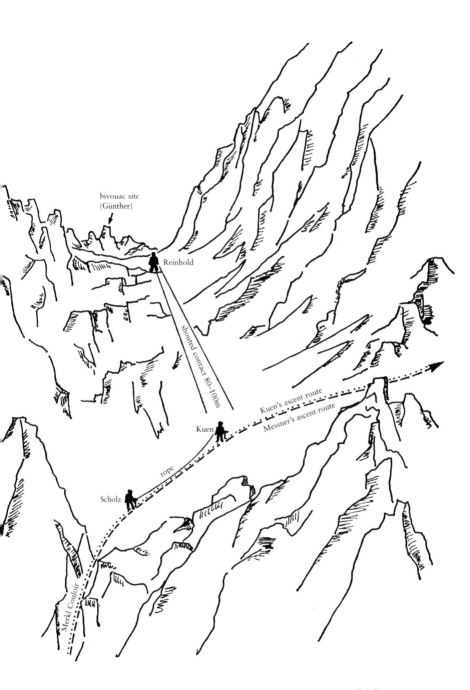

bivouac site
(Günther)

Reinhold

shouted contact 80–100m

Kuen's ascent route

Messner's ascent route

Kuen

rope

Scholz

Merkl Couloir

213

As Felix looked up at me one last time, I shouted and waved to the west, towards the Diamir Face. Felix and Peter were now climbing in our tracks, belaying each other as they went, Felix leading, Peter following. Higher up, they would leave our line of ascent. I took the cord and my gloves and stuffed them in my trouser pockets. In desperation, I went back across to the gap.

What was I supposed to tell Günther? That Felix was going up to the summit and Peter with him? That they hadn't understood me? That at this altitude, in this wind and at a distance of a hundred metres misunderstandings were entirely possible?

Felix later explained to me that he was convinced that everthing really was okay and that he was relieved to be able to carry on to the summit without having to worry about us. He reached the summit of Nanga at four o'clock. Peter arrived a little later. At six o'clock they set off down, bivouacked at 8000m below the South Summit and descended the Merkl Couloir the following morning to Camp 5 and then down to Camp 4. So they would not have passed us even if we had stayed at the Merkl Gap.

Down at Camp 4 people were naturally asking after us; no one knew where we were. Karl did not know and even Felix had no idea. He still had not grasped the fact that after our difficulties in communicating with one another there was only one way out for us: down the Diamir Face.

Down at Base Camp, perplexity and confusion reigned. Information about the summit area was sketchy at best and no one knew if we were still alive. The little information that Herrligkoffer had was insufficient to predict our descent route.

Herrligkoffer: 'First thing in the morning, Günther Messner and Gerd Baur started preparing the ropes to fix the Couloir. Everything got tangled and Günther Messner got angry, threw the ropes down and set off after his brother. Gerd Baur remained at Camp 5. We later heard that he spent the whole day lying in his tent with a sore throat.'

Gerhard Baur then descended to Camp 4 and immediately got on the radio to inform Base Camp of what had happened.

Two days later on 29 June, Felix Kuen and Peter Scholz arrived back at Camp 4. It now became clear that the Messner brothers were somewhere on the Diamir Face but where exactly and why remained a mystery.

Actually we were now on unknown ground, and had been for what seemed an eternity, the victims of cruel fate and desperation. We could not have waited at the Merkl Gap; up there, the only thing waiting for us was death. There had been nothing for it but to attempt to descend the other side of the mountain and somehow just keep going down.

Herrligkoffer, meanwhile, was having the second summit team relate their climb in detail. He wanted to know why Felix had not climbed up to the Merkl Gap.

Kuen: 'We climbed on, putting the rock pitches behind us, before establishing that the uppermost part of the Merkl Couloir would not go. The left-hand side in particular was almost vertical rock and in addition the gully was capped by a cornice. So we traversed right to a series of snow slopes about 100 to 150m below the ridge running up to the top of the wall.'

Once they were that high, Kuen and Scholz would not have been able to see us in any case. Our bivi lay in a blind spot.

Kuen: 'We saw no possibility of helping. At 8000m there is absolutely no sense in heading off into the unknown to look for someone.'

After their bivouac just below the summit Felix and Peter saw nothing more of us. For them we had simply disappeared. For the others we were now lost.

Kuen: 'From our position on the ridge we could look down the face to the Merkl Gap. We listened but we could see nothing and could hear no voices. From the moment that Reinhold waved goodbye, he and Günther had simply vanished.'

To be sure, Kuen and Scholz were worried, but what could they do? The only option was to descend the fixed ropes in the Merkl Couloir to Camp 5 and file a report.

Kuen: 'Grey shadows were creeping up the icefield. I thought of the two men's fast ascent, of their bivouac without equipment, of their descent with no rope into the unknown, of the weak state they must be in.'

Chapter XI

Lost

The summit ridge between the Rupal Face and the Diamir Face. In the background to the left is the Bazhin Gap.

The mighty South Face of Nanga Parbat is the highest mountain face on Earth. Small wonder that the Hindu farmer, looking up from his hard work in the fields at that fearsome wall of ice, believes that the summit above the clouds is the place where all the evil gods gather to send down sickness upon his family, pestilence upon his herds and bad weather upon his harvest.

Fritz Bechtold

The Diamir Face with the Bazhin Gap visible on the left.

The southern flank of Nanga Parbat drops steeply to the Rupal Valley. This 4500m high rock face, with huge hanging glaciers clinging to it, is the highest mountain precipice on Earth. The view from the Bazhin Glacier to the east is the most awe-inspiring view of the entire Nanga Parbat massif.

Karl Maria Herrligkoffer

If you travel from the Eastern Alps to the Western Alps you have to revise your ideas of scale. Going from the Western Alps to bag summits in the Andes you again have to rethink and relearn, although from a mountaineering point of view there are big similarities with the Western Alps region. When you arrive for the first time in the Himalaya, however, you have to deal with a totally different concept of size and scale. The crucial thing here is the large, mutually dependent team, where the lead pair uses the support team as a springboard to the summit and returns after their successful ascent to the waiting arms of their friends at the top camps.

Felix Kuen

Desperate Measures

After the shouted exchange up at the Merkl Gap our situation now looked hopeless. As I made my way back over the snow slope to Günther I was completely beside myself with desperation and bewilderment, shaking and stumbling as I went. I watched myself fall over several times, tearing a hole in my hand with my crampons.

It was almost as if there was a second me up there, as if I was looking down on myself from above. Perhaps I had lost my mind for a moment, lost all contact with reality. I was a split personality, viewing myself in the third person, and the thing was – I did not find it at all unusual.

Wild and conflicting emotions plagued me as I stumbled along. What could we do? I could see no way out now. I knew we were lost, doomed to die. I fell again, rolled down the slope like a bundle of rags, screamed my frustration out, then stood up and suddenly I was calm again.

I can still hear my desperate screams echoing inside my head, even today, but I no longer know why I reacted so savagely. It was as if reason had deserted me, as if all that remained was a body and its animal instincts.

'Now it's you who is crazy,' Günther said, and from the tone of his voice I concluded that he knew he had been acting crazy himself before. It snapped me out of my raging confusion; it was like waking from a terrible nightmare. It was the only time on the whole expedition that I had lost control of myself. Now it was time for action. I knew we had to do something, and fast.

'They are not coming?' my brother asked.

219

'They're going up the other way.'

'Where to?'

'To the summit.'

'And what are we going to do?'

'We can't just do it all again, shouting, waiting and hoping someone comes,' I said with a gesture of hopelessness.

'Then we'll have to go down, Reinhold.' He pointed down into the Diamir Valley. Wisps of cloud were rising up the face. The weather seemed to be getting worse.

'Yes, we've got to get out of here.'

'You've been saying that since this morning.'

'True; but I was hoping help would arrive.'

'We've got to get down.'

'Yes, but where?'

'We have to make a decision now. We should have gone down yesterday.'

If only there hadn't been that slim hope of rescue, we would have been much lower down by now.

But there was no prospect of any help coming now. Any assistance from Felix and Peter could only be expected to arrive the next day at the earliest and from above. They were on the way to the summit and could only get there in the evening. I had seen no one else in the Merkl Couloir and from where we were the descent into the Couloir was out of the question without a rope. I could probably manage to get myself down via the South Summit but that would mean a second bivouac for Günther, on his own this time, and that was unthinkable. Without a stove or a sleeping bag he would never survive it. I did not need to voice this option; I dismissed it out of hand. I could not leave him on his own now.

'It's really easy down there,' Günther pointed straight down. He was right; just easy snow slopes.

'And further down? What will we do if we get stuck down there?'

'We can't stay here. I want to go down.'

'Me too.'

220

The Diamir Face with the descent route marked. The Kinshofer Route takes the ice couloirs on the left.

During those dark and desperate hours I kept thinking of Sigi Löw. I had read that he had died eight years ago at this altitude. Were we now to share his fate? Löw had been a very accomplished rock climber – he was, in name alone, the patron of our expedition – and had reached the summit in 1962 with Toni Kinshofer and Anderl Mannhardt, the most successful German climbers of their time. Like us, they had survived a bivouac at 8000m, similarly equipped with only the bare essentials. Confident that they would return to their top camp the same day, they had set off without sleeping bags. Whilst descending from the bivi, Sigi Löw had lagged behind. He slipped in a harmless, easy snow gully, fell and lay unconscious at the Bazhin Gap. Mannhardt went down to fetch help while Kinshofer stayed with his now semiconscious companion. Löw was confused and suffering terrible hallucinations and could do nothing on his own. Sigi Löw died that evening and Kinshofer descended alone, convinced that he was walking through a tobacco plantation even though, in reality, he was climbing down the endless ice slopes of the top part of the Diamir Face route. Over the following days, the two summiteers suffered severe traumas. Mannhardt and Kinshofer had to be shepherded back to Base Camp. Later they were carried out with frostbitten feet by local porters though the Diamir Valley to the Indus.

Hermann Buhl came to mind again, too. His survival story gave us hope and a little consolation.

Back in 1953, Buhl had spent a night at 8000m standing on a ledge in the freezing cold and the whole of the next day making his descent, all the time at the very limit of his capacity to endure suffering. At one point he had been forced to retrace his steps, 6km in all. Arriving at the Silver Plateau, Buhl could not stay on his feet for exhaustion. He was crawling rather than walking. The fact that he had been the first to reach the summit was the only thing that kept him alive and he fought his way down via the Silver Saddle, victor and vanquished at one and the same time. He came into the top camp like a sleepwalker and his two friends, Dr Frauenberger and Hans Ertl, helped him back to Base Camp. He, too, had suffered frostbitten feet.

Without a rope the Kinshofer Route was much too steep and difficult to down-climb and for a brief moment I considered Buhl's route. But we were already too low and his route would be difficult to find with nothing to mark the way. It was therefore impossible. The Rakhiot descent was the longest and there were huge ice cliffs.

The only ray of hope now was the thought of Mummery's attempt, seventy-five years before us. The route he had tried must be a possible descent route. It was the only way out, our sole remaining escape route. I knew that Mummery had already got beyond the major difficulties when he turned back after spending fourteen days' climbing up and down the 4000m face with his porters. Back then, in 1895, the exit pitch, squeezing between the ice cliffs, had been climbable. Exactly how far Mummery had got was a mystery – perhaps almost as far as the Bazhin Gap – but the dangerous, concave section of the route had presented him with few problems even though there were only two of them at the end, a Gurkha high-altitude porter and Mummery, and they had 1895 equipment!

These thoughts gave me renewed courage. In any case, the choice was simple: attempt to descend or die, frozen to death on the ridge between the two huge faces, the Rupal and the Diamir. Our lives were literally on a knife edge. We had manoeuvred ourselves into a potentially fatal situation and had waited too long for help to arrive.

'If we had known that things would turn out like this', I said to Günther, 'we could have set off down this morning.'

'We waited for nothing.'

'What else could we have done?'

'Gone down the west side straight away.'

'You think so?'

'It would have been more reasonable.'

'Yeah, yeah, right!'

'And we could have spared ourselves that high bivi.'

'We were waiting for the others.'

'Yes, okay. But we have to move fast now. We can't wait here for ever. I can't take another bivouac, Reinhold.'

Descent Into the Unknown

With all other possibilities exhausted, there was now only one route of escape for us: down the Diamir Face. Luckily we had spent the winter studying Nanga Parbat; it had been the

223

obvious thing to do. At home, we had read the books and studied the maps and now had a mental picture of the mountain. These mental images – of the facets of the mountain, the gullies and couloirs and ridges – were our aids to orientation and very valuable when you did not really know where you were going. Knowledge is always an advantage; that also applies when you are on a mountain. For example, I can recognize the Bazhin Gap with just one brief glance, even from above, and after reading about Mummery's attempt I had stored away a mental image of the line of the route as I have since done with thousands of other lines. I now played out the descent of the Mummery Route in my mind's eye. His attempt had been made in 1895, so it was surely possible to down-climb the route now, in 1970, without recourse to artificial aids, I thought. I was sure, too, that Günther would recover as we lost height. From the foot of the face we would somehow make it down to the valley and once we were in the valley we would meet shepherds.

Nevertheless, I was afraid of the descent, very afraid. It was fear of the unknown mostly; straight down the Diamir Face, a 4000m precipice of rock and ice full of unseen dangers and pitfalls. It was certainly a big risk we were taking. For sure, we were young but we were also experienced enough to be scared. We only accepted the risk because there was no other way out and because it would be easier to die trying than do nothing and wait for certain death. I took the first step off the ridge.

It was about 11 o'clock when we started down the Diamir Face. It was a life or death decision. We had no rope, no tent and no food. We had not had anything to drink for forty hours and had hardly eaten a thing. But this was still our only hope, our only chance of survival. Either it worked, or...

One of our companions was later to describe the descent as reckless and my decision as unreasonable and going against the basic principles of mountaineering. I still maintain that it represented the only alternative to certain death.

And we did not want to die – not yet.

I glanced back in the direction of the summit again and looked down into the Merkl Couloir one last time. There was nothing moving down there, and no one to be seen. As we started moving down the snow slopes a feeling of calmness came over us and we suddenly realized that we were doing the only thing possible. The terrain here was not steep and we climbed down facing out.

It was obvious that we would not get far by climbing straight down. We could not just carry on blindly; we had to seek out the best possible line, step by step. I knew full well that although I could guide my brother down I would not be able to lower him down the steep sections without a rope and carrying him was out of the question. But I still had to get him down somehow.

'Do you think we can get down over there by the rocks?'

Günther was looking at me quizzically. 'I reckon so,' he said.

'I'm not so certain.'

'No, nothing is certain.'

'Let me just go on ahead and have a look,' I said.

You can not choose to make a descent like this in the same way as you might, for example, choose a job. There was a feeling of inevitability about it, and I was unable fully to suppress my fear. It was only when I was climbing that this feeling of powerlessness was at all bearable. The inevitable then became just one of many possibilities.

Slowly, very slowly, we went down, traversing below the cliffs of the summit pyramid. The snow was light and soft and we took careful, measured steps. I took the lead, searching for the best route. Whenever I got to a place where I could see a little way ahead I would wait for Günther, who followed me down slowly.

Far below us, a big thunderstorm was building. The clouds were almost black and they were boiling, rising from the Diamir Valley like huge soap bubbles. Occasional

The view of the Diamir Valley from the upper summit headwall.

tatters of mist blew up towards us. The valley floor could not be seen and looking down at the storm clouds was a dizzying experience; it was as if our world had been turned on its head.

Then, out of the blue, a soft hail began to fall. Down below us lightning flashed and thunder rolled and the hailstorm grew heavier. Suddenly, I could no longer see a thing – I could not see the route, or the drop, although I was still aware of it, nor the storm clouds or even the mountain itself. All we could see was the tiny patch of snow we were standing on. Then the clouds parted and the void gaped before us, a bottomless black pit. For a brief moment, as the view cleared, hopefulness was again replaced by helplessness. Beneath us, the face dropped away 3000m clear to the Diamir Valley.

I could wait no longer. I had to go down, have a look, and find a descent route. Finding a way out of this had become an obsession. I carried on down into the mist, occasionally disappearing from Günther's view and then appearing again and waving him down. Fear drove me on down the snow slope, into and out of the patches of cloud. All that mattered now was to try to read the terrain and hope to piece a route together from the fleeting images I had of the mountain, to mend our broken hopes.

Things were now getting steeper and I hoped and prayed that the exit pitch between the seracs, the first crux section, would be negotiable. I had to keep waiting for Günther, who at times was so far above me that I could barely recognize him. He was coming down very slowly. Every step, every hold had to be just right. A single mistake now would spell disaster. Every move had to be deliberately, perhaps even unconsciously executed, but Günther was having trouble concentrating. Finally, he joined me.

'You doing all right?' I asked him.

'Yes, but it's slow going. Where to next?' he asked after a while.

'It'll be okay. You hungry?'

'No.'

'You must eat something,' I said.

'I'm thirsty, that's all.'

'You want one of these Multibionta vitamin tablets?'

'Have you got any water?'

'No, but I'll make some. Have a bit of that energy food while you're waiting. I've still got a few crumbs left in my jacket pocket.'

I rummaged around in my pockets and found two tins. Emptying one of them, I dropped the remaining vitamin tablets in the other and pocketed it. I stuck one tablet in the empty tin and stuffed it full of snow. Then I held it in my bare hands and blew on it. The vitamin tablet slowly dissolved and started frothing. I had produced two sips of ice-cold liquid. Günther drank them down with his eyes shut.

The Diamir Face. Below and to the left of centre is the egress between the seracs.

We continued our descent; two tiny dots in the mist, lost on an endless snow slope. Random images of Günther and of this vertical world kept flooding into my mind. To anyone who might have been flying over the face, we would have looked like ghosts. A short while later I found myself standing between two huge ice cliffs, shooting up into the mists, the size of skyscrapers. If we could find a way between them we might yet be saved. That way maybe? No! But finally, miraculously, I did find the narrow gap through the big band of seracs. Immediately below the ice was hard and smooth. There was only this one route down. Instinct took over and we stayed off the ice and kept to a blunt rib of rock alongside.

228

The Third Man

I felt like a tiny dot on the landscape as we moved between the seracs and into uncharted territory below. Down we went, zig-zagging to avoid the cliffs and constrictions. Two huge seracs, each more than 50m high, hung suspended on the steep face above us, between them a shimmering blue wall of hard ice inlaid with little islands of rock. I went on ahead, disappeared from Günther's view beneath a cliff and popped up again further left before detouring around a crevasse and coming to a stop. I waved and shouted for Günther to follow.

It was only by staying ahead and getting an overall view of the terrain that I was able to spare Günther the agony of false trails and additional ascents, but the route was not easy to find and I often had to climb back up a good way. On one section the front points of our crampons were only biting a few millimetres deep into the glassy hard ice. You could hear clearly the noise the pick of the axe made as it hit the ice. At times our whole weight was on our crampons and axes.

Suddenly there was a third climber next to me. He was descending with us, keeping a regular distance a little to my right and a few steps away from me, just out of my field of vision. I could not see the figure and still maintain my concentration but I was certain there was someone there. I could sense his presence; I needed no proof. Certain sounds seemed to confirm his presence: a creaking of the ice, a noise of some kind. He did not speak; he was simply there. He stopped when I stopped; he climbed when I climbed. Maybe I was being followed by a ghost. Whatever it was, I was sure it was there and the mere presence somehow helped me regain my composure.

So now we were three. I never stopped to ask myself how that could be; it just was. Later I told myself no, it could not be; it was just the two of us, Günther and me, on our own; that I had been seeing things; that the figure could not have

229

been there. Then, suddenly, there it was again, climbing down alongside me and maintaining a regular distance from us.

It was evening when we reached the first continuous stretch of rocks. There were lighter patches here and there – remnants of ice. Where previously it had been scattered outcroppings of rock amongst the smooth ice, it was now isolated shields of ice between the rocks – a world in black and white. I was taking my gloves off more and more often now, in order to get a better grip.

The only thing I could now do for Günther was to find the best way down and to wait for him to catch up. The climbing he had to deal with on his own.

'Where's your other glove, Günther?' I asked as he joined me.

'You've got it.'

'How's that?'

'You said you'd bring it with you.'

'I came down before you, though.'

'I must have lost it somewhere then.'

'Where?'

'I don't know.'

He had probably left it lying somewhere and simply forgotten it. I had a reserve pair and gave them to him. I still had two pairs of mittens; that was enough.

A little way below the seracs it began to get dark. I headed for a buttress of rock I could see a little way further down. I could clearly see the upper part of the Mummery Rib.

'We could stay here, Reinhold,' Günther suggested during a rest break.

'For now, maybe. But not until the morning. Too dangerous.'

'I'm tired. We need to rest.'

'We can't.'

'Why not?'

'It's in the line of fire here.'

'Why?'

'Because of those seracs above us.'

'Oh, yes.'

'We have to carry on down.'

Although it was now night, we could still see. At this altitude, when the sky is clear, the light from the stars is enough to see your way by and our eyes had also got used to the dark. Feet first, heads bowed, we crawled down over the rocks like four-legged creatures, losing height centimetre by centimetre. We could hear the seracs creaking and groaning under their own weight and held our breath at the repeated whirring sounds as slivers of ice broke away and plummeted down the face. Now and then a larger lump went whistling by into the void but the danger could not been seen, only heard. Occasionally we could smell the sulphur in the cold night air. Günther kept his head held high; perhaps he could sense the danger.

Second Bivouac

Down at Base Camp they would be standing around the campfire, shadowy figures in the night. The mood would be subdued, I imagined.

We did not waste much time trying to imagine what the others would be doing, however. We were far too busy trying to survive. At midnight we started sorting out our second bivouac, somewhere on the upper part of the Mummery Rib. I wasn't thinking much, just the odd fleeting thought of home. All of a sudden I heard water splashing, a spring flowing out of the ice perhaps. I was so thirsty.

I went off for a look but returned to our bivi with nothing. The ice was still frozen solid; I must have been hearing things. A short while later I heard it again, a faint gurgling noise. Perhaps I was imagining things again.

It was now getting lighter. We could make out individual rock features, so the moon must be up. It was a waxing moon and cast a silvery light onto the face.

'Günther,' I said and prodded him. I had decided to descend a little further and was just waiting for an answer from him. We had to get down the most dangerous part of the wall as fast as possible if we were to make it to the foot of the face before sunrise.

Günther took a while getting to his feet. Awkwardly, he grabbed his axe, searched for something else, then picked it up. Everything happened very slowly. Presently, he was wide awake too; no longer half dead with fatigue, thirst and hunger, he did not seem nearly as confused now.

The descent by moonlight seemed eerie and strange. We climbed down a rock buttress and over some big detached blocks, keeping to the line of the Mummery Rib, with occasional excursions onto the ice at the side. We seemed to be instinctively aware of the safety aspect and whenever one of our crampons skittered and slipped we would immediately look to see that nothing had happened. I soon reached another platform, where I waited for Günther. Bent double, with one hand clutching the rock, we leaned out and looked down, trying to decide on the best route. What was it to be – left or right?

I was feeling cold and short on words, so I pointed with my axe to the left. 'okay?'

'Okay.' Günther motioned with his chin towards a steep gully. I nodded, then, without a word, I set off climbing again. Günther watched me go and then made as if to follow me down. He shouted and I answered 'Yes, it's loose down here. Wait a minute. Watch out!' Günther stood on the platform, freezing, the hood of his anorak pulled up over his cap, his glacier goggles hanging loosely around his neck, ice axe in hand. His legs were bent. They looked about to collapse. He was so tired, his face was ashen grey. Finally came the shout he was waiting for:

'Come on down!'

232

No answer. Günther gazed down into the gully, but the gully was empty.

'Günther! Climb when you're ready!' I shouted again. The voice snapped him out of his reverie.

I was standing in a little niche out of the fall line and peered cautiously around the arête. I waited until Günther arrived. We were battle weary now, tired and worn out but still strung out, tense and nervous. I moved off again, hesitantly at first, down rock steps, gullies and loose blocks. The terrain was steeper now and did not look as if it was getting any easier. How far was it to the glacier now? Then, quite suddenly, the climbing seemed easy and safe, like in a dream.

'I've climbed this thing before,' I said to Günther.

'You can't have done.'

'This bit exactly. I know where every hold is.'

'Impossible.'

'I climbed it exactly the same way last time I did it.'

'I'm telling you we've never been here before.'

'Then it must have been somewhere else. I don't know where. Maybe on another mountain. But I have climbed this pitch before, I'm sure of it.'

'You can't have done.'

But the feeling of being on a familiar route persisted. I was surprised at the way the moves seemed to flow automatically, as if I had committed the sequences to memory or replayed them over and over again in my dreams. My guardian angel was with me again.

No Reply

We had reached the easy-angled gully at the lower end of the upper section of the Mummery Rib. The major difficulties were behind us and I was moving faster now, hoping to get down to the glacier before the sun hit the face. Günther was somewhere above me; I knew he was there without turning to look. We were moving together down the hard firn slopes, crampons biting nicely and all the crevasses clearly visible. It looked as if our problems were over. Günther seemed much fresher than yesterday; obviously he had recovered a little. In spite of everything, we had cracked it!

We heard later that we were supposed to have planned the complete traverse of Nanga Parbat from the start. How else could we have found the way down the Diamir Face? I did not know at the time how simple the solution to a seemingly impossible set of problems can appear after the event. People naturally questioned how we had been able to get down the mountain without a plan. But there never had been a plan.

We headed down the huge concave slope between the Diamir Face and the Mazeno Face, dodging between the ice falls and heading for the sanctuary of the valley below. We each chose the line that best suited us, one of us going left to avoid a steep section, the other heading round to the right. I kept waiting for Günther and shouted up to him, not knowing if he could hear me; 'We have to hurry. We've got to get down before the sun comes on to the face because of the avalanche danger!'

'Are we going to head down there to the right, between the seracs?'

The ice looked quite broken there.

'Yes. It will be the fastest way down.' It looked as if we could reach the green below by going right between the seracs. 'We'll wait for each other at the first spring.'

I was climbing faster now, convinced that Günther had understood. There were no more serious obstacles and all I wanted to do now was get down before it was too late.

Nothing more could happen to us now, I thought, even though we were totally out of it and exhausted to the point of apathy.

The concave face to the right of the lowest part of the Mummery Rib.

Günther had his ice axe in his hand. The snow beneath his boots was frozen hard and his crampons had worked loose. He hesitated, standing there for a moment unsure of which way to go, then followed me down. Everything was quiet now; the calm of the early morning hours. Actually, for all I knew it might well have been the late afternoon. I just kept on going, heading down between the ice cliffs. Günther would be fine; he couldn't miss the route now and he wasn't going to fall into any crevasses. Mummery had not even bothered with a rope here. The difficulties were well and truly over.

'This is like a motorway,' I thought as I started out across an avalanche chute to the left. I instinctively knew that descending the avalanche debris would be less strenuous. On the dead glacier further over to the right and directly below the Diamir Face there were more crevasses, with seracs above. My route seemed the better one. To the right, where we had originally intended to come down, there was a mass of big rocks to trip over. The second option was now the best.

Günther had not appeared but it was nothing to worry about as I knew I would not be able to see him from where I was. He must be on the plateau by now, or close to it, I thought. There was a big hump between us so we were out of sight of each other but I was sure Günther would come into view soon and did not really think much more about it. The avalanche chute I had used was easy to follow.

The sun was up now. Its light slowly filled the high corrie at the head of the Diamir Valley. It immediately started getting warmer. Rays of sunlight strafed the slopes of the Mazeno Ridge as the first avalanches began to thunder down the faces. Where was Günther? The glacier began to flow with rivulets of water. I chopped a small hollow in the ice, lay down and drank without stopping. I was insatiable.

I was incredibly tired now and stayed where I was for a while, resting and drinking. This was the fourth day without shelter or water and I hoped Günther was also drinking the meltwater. Again and again I knelt down and drank, occasionally pausing to look back up the mountain. Günther was still nowhere to be seen.

After gulping down the glacier water I felt as heavy as lead, tired and apathetic. I consoled myself with the thought that Günther must have gone down the other way. 'Over there, between the seracs,' I heard myself say. He would be sitting down at one of the little rivulets drinking his fill like I had just done. And the dead glacier was fairly easy terrain. No, I wasn't worried about Günther; not yet.

After an extended rest I continued my descent. The sun and the large quantity of water I had guzzled had worn me out. I was moving hunched over like an old man, dragging my feet, taking short steps. I often stopped and looked up for any sign of Günther but Günther was still nowhere to be seen.

'He'll be up ahead somewhere, down amongst the greenery drinking spring water,' I thought. Spring water – the thought of it quickly became an obsession.

'He must have gone down over there,' I kept repeating to myself over and over again. It was like a mantra, a prayer that I would find him, and a consolation for me at one and the same time. He would be sitting by a spring waiting for me. I had to hurry. Maybe his route down had been shorter.

The best way across to the lateral moraines was not immediately obvious. I was now stumbling across a dead glacier, dislodging stones with my boots that rolled downhill and splashed into the pools of meltwater. High up on the wall, I could hear the roar of an avalanche. I came to a little glacial stream, lay my ice axe on the ground and stretched out to drink some more. Then I sat on a rock. I was dead tired. I thought I could hear voices. One voice calling my name and others talking to me in whole sentences, although I could only understand fragments of what they were saying. I felt lightheaded and could feel the light

At the foot of the Diamir Face. The two descent routes are marked. (I = ice avalanche).

behind my closed eyelids. So many voices! All speaking at once. My mother's voice was also there. The voices babbled along like a stream, like trickles of meltwater. They whispered, murmured and called my name over and over again:

'Reinhold!'

I looked around, curious to see this strange presence. Bewildered, I got to my feet and there he was again, the lone climber. But no, it wasn't Günther. Günther was not there; he must have taken the higher route.

Awkwardly, I reached for my axe and stumbled off again. The voices were silent for a while but as I reached the edge of the moraine they were back again. And there were people, too, waiting for me – no doubt about it. Further left I could see a horse; yes, a horse. They were coming nearer. They must have seen me, I thought. Then the horse stopped. And the others? Surely it was too early for a search party?

238

At first I thought it might be another expedition and then, beyond the moraine, I saw some cattle. Shepherds with their herds, perhaps? I stumbled onwards across the dead glacier, stepping over crevasses, heading towards the edge of the moraine but was disappointed to see that there was no one there waiting for me. The horse turned out to be a crevasse, the people just clumps of bushes and stones. The cattle I had seen earlier were boulders scattered amongst the grass.

The last steep uphill slope sapped nearly all my remaining energy. The steep and unstable scree was hard work and I often had to stop and rest, slumped over almost unconscious, before hauling myself upright again and climbing a little higher. I clung to clumps of grass, slipping and scrabbling for secure footholds and trying not to give up. But I couldn't manage it, not in my state. I was wrecked.

It was quite pathetic, really, but I could find little humour in the situation. Whenever I instructed my legs to move they simply disobeyed orders. I tried crawling but even this most basic animal function seemed beyond me. I was nearing the end and the only thing that kept me going was the thought that I must find the spring where Günther would be waiting for me. He must be somewhere out here. I gritted my teeth and kept going.

A little while later I found myself standing in a large green hollow with a few big boulders in the middle. It would have made a perfect campsite. I found a few empty tins and presumed that the place had been used as a base camp by an earlier Diamir Face expedition. I had a look around, wandered about a bit listening for the sound of water and actually did find a freshwater spring. But not my brother. I took a drink and had another look around, feeling suddenly uneasy.

Where was Günther?

'Günther!' I shouted.

There was no reply.

I walked slowly over to one of the boulders in the middle of the meadow and took off my heavy boots. It was very hot

View from the freshwater spring towards the foot of the Face.

now. I walked barefoot back to the spring and sat there for a while gulping down water. Günther would be here any minute now, I thought. We had survived.

I dipped my feet in the cold water and then had a wash. I kept looking over to the glacier. Nothing. An hour had passed and Günther was still not here. I did not know what to do. I shouted, whistled and kept lookout but there was still no sign of him.

I was feeling pretty anxious by now so I pulled my boots, shirt and trousers on again, left the rest of my stuff at the boulder and wandered off up the valley to look for him. I searched amongst the pools of water and the streams, going right up to the edge of the Diamir Glacier before turning round and retracing my steps back to the boulder, which was a kind of point of reference for me.

Günther was not there – still not there.

I walked down the valley for a good half hour but there was still no sign of him. Suddenly I started to panic and hurried back as best I could to the campsite, grabbed my axe and headed back up the glacier the way I had come down.

If someone had ordered me to go back up again a few hours previously I would not have been able to do it. Now, however, my tiredness had evaporated, the hard graft long forgotten. I had to find my brother! He could not have simply disappeared. 'I have to go back and find him' – the thought hammered in my head.

The snow had now softened up. The sun was beating down and reflecting off the glacier as I struggled through the slushy snow in the avalanche chute I had come down, often sinking in up to my knees. The snow had been hard packed here but now my trousers and boots were soaked, everything was dripping wet and the meltwater trickled into my inner boots. I was not bothered; the thought of finding Günther kept me going. Slowly, I slogged back up the avalanche debris to the plateau. It was there that I had last seen Günther.

There was no sign of his tracks, or of mine either. In the morning the snow had been hard and we had left few tracks as we descended the slopes to the foot of the wall but now I could neither see nor hear anything. I was aware only of an emptiness inside and a feeling of loss and hopelessness.

I kept an eye out for holes in the snow but found no open crevasses. I shouted, but got no answer. I had no idea what could have happened to him. I kept on searching, desperate by now. I was looking for my brother, for an alternative descent route, for answers. It was becoming hopeless.

The sun was setting as I finally decided to descend to the foot of the Diamir Face. If Günther had not followed me this was the only route he could have taken. And he could not have followed me, or I would have seen him.

The Avalanche

All of a sudden I stumbled across the debris from an avalanche: a chaotic jumble of lumps of ice and powder snow. Huge blocks of ice, some the size of cupboards, lay scattered and piled beneath a vertical band of tottering seracs. A little shaken at first, I just stood and stared at the sheer quantity of ice that had fallen. Then the shock and disbelief set in. I simply could not believe that Günther might be lying buried beneath the debris, that he might be dead. It was inconceivable that he had been passing this way at the exact moment the serac had collapsed – inconceivable and therefore impossible.

It was dark now as I absent-mindedly stumbled down a trough somewhere between the Diamir and the Diama glaciers. Günther had to be here somewhere. I was going to look for him and I promised myself I was going to find him.

In between the whistling of the wind, I kept thinking I could hear footsteps. He must be here. And there was Günther's voice, too; he had to be somewhere near. I followed the voice and this feeling I had, long-since oblivious to the massive balcony of creaking and tottering ice that hung above my head.

The whole world was suddenly in a state of suspended animation. Everything was dead, the stones frozen to the ice. Silence reigned. At the edge of the glacier I could make out something large – the lateral moraines probably – and, to the left and right, an unbroken band of ice cliffs. My ghostly third man was there, too, seemingly lost amongst the seracs and the debris of old ice.

'…down there to the right, between the seracs.'

Those had been Günther's last words. I heard him mumble that one sentence over and over again and even mouthed it myself. Now I went back up the dead glacier, wandering aimlessly in circles like a mad man. Perhaps I really was mad.

As I walked I saw my mother at home, my mother in the kitchen, my brothers in the yard, then my mother again. She just stood there and looked at me. Günther? Had he just disappeared? It could not be true.

It was too late now, I told myself. There was no point looking for him any more. He must have been buried under the avalanche. I could not help him; not any more.

We had often set off climbing together, just the two of us, often on long and difficult routes, and we had always returned together. I still could not accept that Günther was now missing. I had to find him. How could I possibly return home without him?

'Günther!' I shouted again.

Had I not dreamed last winter of coming down alone from Nanga Parbat to an empty base camp? At the time, I had not attached any particular significance to the dreams; after all, I had read all the books about Nanga Parbat. Nowadays I find myself wondering sometimes whether it really was all that stored information that had sent me off into the world I had dreamed of or whether something else had been at work.

'Günther!'

With every noise I made, the silence grew louder and the dangers of the glacial world around me seemed to grow more threatening.

'Günther!'

Somehow I managed to keep going. Presently, my path was blocked by a crevasse so I retraced my steps and soon arrived back at the scene of the avalanche. I could hear the ice creaking and groaning and the clatter of a stone as it slid into a crevasse. I stumbled over large plates of ice piled randomly on top of each other, then stopped again.

'Günther!' I shouted.

It was the anguished cry of a lost animal.

I spent the whole of that night wandering around aimlessly, shouting, falling asleep, waking up freezing and shouting again, feeling powerless and desperately alone. In the morning I went down. I had run out of places to look and did not know what to do. Strung out by lack of sleep and anxiety, I drifted into unconsciousness.

When I awoke I was completely drained. I felt groggy, as if I was coming round after a general anaesthetic, as if I had forgotten everything. My head felt as if it was full of cotton wool, my brain numb. I could not even cry. I was unsure of who I really was. Summoning my last vestiges of reason, I managed to understand that the third man was just me watching myself from a different plane of existence.

The avalanche debris was still in shadows. 'Günther!' I shouted again, but there was only silence. The sun was bathing the tops of the Mazeno ridge and the weather seemed to be improving. High up the valley the first blue plumes of morning mist were rising. I wondered how far away from any other people I was.

'Günther!' My shouts were pure reflex now.

The other climber was back again but he no longer had a voice. He came down the avalanche chute, ice axe in hand, and headed for the valley. He glanced back but there was nothing moving, no sign of life, nothing. The sun was shining down on the valley.

But it was not shining for me.

As if in a trance, I watched the third man as he made his descent, stumbling along, searching for a route between the seracs. Ice axe clenched in his hand, his eyes screwed up into narrow slits, he swayed and staggered on the ice. The skin hung in tatters from his nose. His lips and eyes were badly swollen. He seemed to be moving automatically, without thinking.

I had been making my way down since the sun had come onto the Diamir Face. I had no idea where I was going. I was apathetic, aimless, empty. I felt as if I had forgotten everything. I had never been on Nanga Parbat – no, never – and Günther had never existed. There had never been anyone here, not even me. I felt ready to die. There was no reason

244

Nanga Parbat from the west. The foot of the Face and the Diamir Valley are in shadow.

to keep going, no point in searching any longer, no reason to live. My legs were too weak to carry me; my throat was raw, my voice gone. Still with no answers to the questions that Günther had posed during the night, I began to die.

The realization that I was dying dawned slowly. Yet although I could hear nothing but the sound of my own breathing, somewhere in my subconscious mind the third climber was still present.

He reached the campsite. He took off his shirt, then his boots. His socks were wet. He bent down and took them off. Suddenly he sat bolt upright. His toes were blue. His trousers fell around his ankles, and he massaged his feet.

I spread my clothes out on the boulder in the sun to dry. They smelled of sweat and grit and death and ice.

My feet were frozen and numb but there was little I could do. I walked barefoot over to the spring, squatted down and bathed my feet in the icy cold water.

The pain was not yet bad and although I was very weak, walking was bearable; losing Günther was not. My frostbitten feet were not really a problem, I told myself; they would be okay; they wouldn't stay blue forever.

I slept for a few hours and when I awoke the sun was high in the sky. I kept looking around, expecting someone to come. Günther, maybe? Maybe, but I was also expecting to see my companions from Base Camp. As evening came, I was still alone.

Meanwhile, over at Base Camp they were getting very concerned. There was talk of sending out a search party. Herrligkoffer was running through various scenarios in his mind, but the big question remained: how could anyone manage to get back down the Diamir Face to the valley with no equipment and no support? Surely it was impossible?

Kuen: 'The expedition leadership was perplexed about the fact that the Messner brothers still had not turned up. We had no way of knowing how their adventure, their little prank, had turned out. There was no praise due. They had not even been equipped to basic alpine standards. One thing was certain: they had failed to keep to the agreed plan and had thus alienated themselves from our company.'

Meanwhile, back at 'the rock' in the upper Diamir Valley, I was getting ready to bivouac. I crawled under an overhang and lay down, exhausted. The hunger, the frostbitten toes and the cold no longer troubled me.

I could see no real reason to continue, except in order to let our parents and all the others at home know what had happened, my mother above all. But to walk out alone was out of the question. And I did not want to arrive home alone. It was something I simply could not imagine doing.

246

That night I slept little, as I had done on the three previous bivouacs, alternating between dozing a little and falling into a death-like state of unconsciousness.

I still could not accept that I was on my own, that Günther was dead. We had spent so much time together. All in all, we had spent forty days and forty nights together on Nanga Parbat. I now felt the closeness and the harmony we had enjoyed like never before. It had only been our normal daily life and our habits that had prevented me from seeing Günther as the ideal climbing partner.

I watched the blades of grass before my eyes as they shivered in the chill early morning breeze. It got colder and I sat up. A bright new morning was dawning over the mountain. I was still alive.

The air was almost still. Silence and light played across the mountains. I breathed deeply. This new day would be a new beginning, I thought.

I was sadder now than I had been yesterday, more lost and alone than a solo astronaut on the moon. Never before had I been so far away from other people.

'Günther!' I called his name again and again. It had become a habit.

By the time the sun had reached the foot of the Diamir Face I had decided on a course of action, although it felt like it was someone else who was making the decision. The third climber and I had become one and the same person.

One of us bundled all the spare clothing into the anorak and knotted the arms together. He pushed the ice axe through and hoisted the bundle onto his shoulder, took one last look around and left. After a few steps he stopped. Perhaps they would be sending a helicopter?

All I could think about was rescue.

I watched again as one of us walked back over to the boulder and rummaged about in his bundle until he found a red nylon gaiter, which he placed on the rock and weighted with stones. The gaiter hung like a pennant in the sun.

Looking up the Diamir Face of Nanga Parbat.

It was my sign, the only one I could think of leaving for the search party. I had no pencil with which to write a note, so it would have to do.

Return Through the Diamir Valley

Again I watched myself pick up my bundle of clothes, glance back at the gaiter flapping in the wind, the sign that I was alive, and leave.

The dead glacier ran for 10km down into the valley. The right-hand bank was a strip of bright green meadow flecked with tiny meltwater streams. Above, the rocky flanks of the mountain rose steeply. Amongst the tangle of grass bushes,

248

not far from the lateral moraine, a figure was making his lonely way down into the valley. He was exhausted, crawling on his hands and knees. He stopped at a dry stream bed and looked around as if waiting for someone or searching for something. He listened to the silence and then set off again, crawling down the stony bed of the stream, shouting for his brother. But there was no one else there.

My feet were burning, my throat thick with mucous. My legs would not carry me any longer. I crawled on like a wounded animal, heading aimlessly down the valley, a man without a purpose, driven only by the will to survive. I could only hope that I would meet someone soon. 'Just keep going', I said to myself, ' They must be coming soon.' I was talking to myself a lot now. It seemed to help. I could not just sit down and wait to die. No, sitting down would be too dangerous; I would have fallen asleep for ever. And I did not want the others to miss me. So I kept going.

There was a rock the size of a chair in the middle of the stream bed and next to it a little puddle of clear water. I sat down awkwardly, took off my boots and my socks and wiggled my toes, grimacing with pain. My feet were badly swollen, the toes blue. I dipped the useless lumps of meat into the water to cool them down.

It was the wrong thing to do and I knew it. But the soles of my feet were burning and there was a painful pressure near the toes, as if they were about to burst. I could not help myself. I was thirsty, too – dreadfully thirsty – and hungry.

I did not want the others to go past without seeing me, so I kept shouting. 'Hello!' I shouted. 'Hello!' Without help I doubted that I would make it.

Why did I not just sit where I was and do nothing? Because I had to make it home. My mother knew nothing of Günther's death and my mother could not be left in the dark.

Much later I came across an abandoned hamlet; just a few scattered huts at the bottom of a cliff face. There was nobody

The dead glacier with the route across to the Rupal Valley in the background.

around. I did not stop to wonder how long the place had been deserted. Years ago there must have been a rock fall, I thought; the roofs of the huts were all smashed, the walls had collapsed and the ground was peppered with deep holes. Only two or three of the houses had escaped undamaged. I shouted. There was no one there to answer.

The temptation to give up and sit down was overwhelming. Yes, dying would now be easier, I thought. But I wanted to go home, so I had to carry on.

After half an hour's rest I watched dispassionately as someone vaguely familiar crawled down the glacial moraine. He was bent almost double now, making painfully slow progress through the endless sea of rocks. Minute by minute, hour by hour, he kept on going, leaning against the bigger boulders, slipping and falling, then getting up again, crawling on his hands and knees. He fell to the ground a hundred times and a hundred times he dragged himself to his feet again, picked up his bundle and went on. More and more often now, he just lay there staring before finally struggling to his feet. That someone was me.

Where were the people? I had to find some people – and soon. I did not know on which side of the glacier I would find anyone but I did know that I had to get to the nearest village as fast as possible without missing the others on the way. Surely there must be a search party out by now? I knew that without food or shelter I was finished, but I had already accepted the fact that I might die and was no longer frightened or repulsed by the idea. Death had been my constant companion for days now. But I still had not given up. I kept moving.

I was plagued by doubts – about the route, about myself, about everything. Would my companions ever come?

How far would my will still carry me, if there was nobody out looking for me? I did not want to drag myself up the next hill of moraine for nothing; not now, when I could ill afford to make any detours. I would sooner have kept on going downhill but I thought I had heard people on the other side of the glacier and I needed to take a look.

I scrambled up the pile of scree and rubble, feet slipping even in my heavy black mountain boots. My bad foot was swollen and my boots too tight, so I took off one of the boots and tried barefoot. My foot was bleeding, I slipped again and fell, catching hold of a bush to keep my balance.

I was so tired. But I was not yet ready to sit down and die.

I watched as if in a dream as the lone climber traversed across and up the hillock, kicking footholds in the rubble with one boot, dragging his bare and injured foot behind him. Blood seeped from the cuts. He was barely moving now, his progress measured in centimetres, yet he still refused to give up.

'If only I could let the others know where I am,' I thought before sinking to the ground again, exhausted and dizzy.

When I awoke it was afternoon; I must have been lying there unconscious for several hours.

'Keep going!' I heard a voice telling me and all at once I knew that I had to do just that. Not because it was so late in the day – time had ceased to exist for me; there was only day and night – but because I had a duty to fulfil: to get home

251

and tell my mother what had happened.

The lone climber got to his feet, picked up his things and set off again. He followed the upper edge of the lateral moraine at first, then dropped down, heading for the trees, and vanished into the undergrowth. He was wandering through a faraway world, barefoot, in a trance.

Why were they not coming? Base Camp was not that far away!

I felt sorry for my friends at Base Camp. They had no way of knowing what had happened to us.

Presently I came to a clearing. The grass had been grazed and that meant cattle. I suddenly felt a little more hopeful.

He dragged himself over to the clearing and stood for a while, a shadowy figure in the open expanse of grazing land. In the centre of the meadow there was a big rock and next to it stood a hut. A little way below the hut there were cows grazing. And was that a man he could see? It was!

I stood spellbound at the edge of the clearing, trying to convince myself that I was saved. Was that really a person over there? I had been waiting so long for this moment that the image now seemed unreal. I had grown afraid of my hallucinations and was no longer sure what was real and what was merely a figment of my imagination. In the state I was in now, I would not have been able to cope with yet another disappointment. I think I would have just sat down and died.

'Hello!' Was that someone shouting?

I shouted as best I could but the figure walked into the trees and disappeared from view. I could not see anyone else around. Desperate now, I shouted again, louder this time, but the person – a local farmer perhaps – did not return. I could only hope it really was a person.

For a moment I thought I had been mistaken but the cows and the trees were still there, so I could not have been hallucinating. Then, suddenly, I saw more people, real people, not just shadowy figures or spirits of the air, so close I could almost reach out and touch them.

252

Chapter XII

Death and Rebirth

The Diamir Valley below Nanga Parbat.

The elation at our victory remains muted.

Felix Kuen

I also died, at least once, on the way down from
Nanga Parbat. Returning to civilization was like a
rebirth for me. I had spent weeks in the cold, in thin
air, and in great danger. After days in complete
isolation, I came across some local people. The images
I saw – a pony man, signposts, pools of water – all
faded as fast as they had appeared.

Reinhold Messner

The Mazeno Pass, a possible route between the Rupal Valley and the Diamir Valley.

The Messner brothers, Peter Scholz and I, successfully completed the third ever ascent of Nanga Parbat. It was the first time that seven climbers had scaled the 4500m Rupal Face, the highest mountain face in the world. Four of us reached the summit but the Messners are still missing. The last thing we heard was when Reinhold shouted to us that they would be taking a different route down.

Felix Kuen

The Messners blatantly broke the number one rule, never to indulge in extravagances.

Karl Maria Herrligkoffer

Hallucinations

Base camp is in turmoil. Naturally, everyone is concerned. Karl makes sure the slopes to the left of the Rupal Face are searched, and justifies his stance by reiterating that Günther was not fit to summit: 'I had my reasons for not lining Günther up for the summit,' Herrligkoffer said.

Our worlds are now at opposite poles. Whilst I am on the one side of the mountain, working my way down towards the valley, at times even crawling, plagued by hallucinations, my feet in all sorts of trouble, on the other side of the mountain, Herrligkoffer is preparing his retreat. The expedition is over. I still live in hope that somebody will look for me and maybe even find me. How my companions are meant to find their way into the Diamir Valley, I have no idea.

How are they meant to know where to look? Günther and I split up from the rest of the team.

'Because the Messner brothers cannot make their way back down the ascent route' was the reason given by Herrligkoffer when ordering all camps to be cleared. It was true. We were not likely to reappear on the Rupal Face. If we had stayed in our first bivouac, then we would have been dead days ago. A descent down the Merkl Couloir or anywhere else on the Rupal Face would have been out of the question.

My own reality is very different. I am so far away from everything: the expedition, the mountain and our home.

Lying there unconscious for a few hours, I felt fine. Everything seemed so easy. My life, a mere dream I once had. The hopes and fears of the last few days appeared and drifted away, like film clips. I could not keep the images in my head and I was unable to make any sense of the conflicting

255

emotions washing over me. In my confusion, I began talking to myself. Perhaps it was so that I did not feel quite so alone. And Günther was there again. He was with me the whole way down the mountain. He even talked back to me. One of those serious statements he used to make springs to mind: 'The oldies are wrong when they talk of the good old days. When you are young, everything is serious and difficult, and nobody gives you a helping hand.'

The only fragments of memories I have of my experiences then, are like snap-shots, frozen moments, with no context whatsoever. Günther, for example, complains of a loose crampon as though I had given him lousy equipment.

Still quite high up on the Diamir Face, we see a hut. It lies just to the right of the glacier, in a green patch. A voice says we must go there.

As I get there two days later and find I am walking round a pile of rocks I am not even surprised. It was as though my subconscious could easily deal with these distortions of reality.

Further down in the valley, on the dead glacier, I spot a wooden pole. Once there, not even a trace of such an item is to be seen.

And did I not see a horse over there in the snow?

No, it is just a glacial table.

Ah, but now I definitely see a herd of cattle in front of me. I get closer. No, those dark patches are boulders and are not moving. A rockslide must have come down here years ago.

But just before, I am sure I saw a man disappear into the woods did I not?

Yes, there *is* a man! Does he really exist?

The first person Reinhold Messner met in the Diamir Valley.

The First People

As if from nowhere, one of them comes towards me through a meadow bursting with flowers. He stops at the hut by the stone pile and calls out. He looks and shouts, again and again, but he gets no answer. He then throws a stone at the roof of the hut. Still no response. He decides to leave. He stops again where he had originally stood. There is a regular sound of banging somewhere. Someone is chopping wood.

I went there and saw some people. Three men, chopping wood! No mistake, these were locals. I was no longer alone. But were these men real? It was only when I grabbed one of the woodcutters that I knew they were.

I start to talk to them in pidgin English, but I can tell from their expressions that they do not understand a single word I say. I sit down next to a felled tree. I am so

257

exhausted I cannot stand anymore. Two of the men come and sit with me, another remains standing, constantly shaking his head, as though he just cannot get what the link might be between his world and mine.

He wants to know where this foreigner comes from.

So I take a fist-sized stone and place it on the ground, to represent Nanga. In the simplest way, I trace our route up the mountain with my finger and then show them the way down into the Diamir Valley. All three of them look at me with blank faces. How on earth could one man get across the mountain on his own? The standing man says 'eg' and raises his thumb. It means 'one'. Does he want to know if I am alone?

How can I explain to him that there were two of us but that Günther died en route?

I show him two fingers, the victory sign, and then close my eyes to communicate my loss.

They understand and avert their eyes.

I clumsily try to give them further details with sign language and drawings in the dirt. That's right, my expedition team is on the other side of the mountain. I try to find out if anyone has been here, looking for me. Bit by bit, the locals get a clearer picture of my situation. I can see it in their eyes. An hour later, they realize that I am hungry. The woodcutters give me a piece of chapatti, a thin round flat loaf. It is cold and has not been salted and tastes woody.

Although it is only a small piece, it is the first bit of proper food I have eaten in five days and I nearly choke on it.

I cannot eat any more. Just chewing makes me want to vomit and I can barely swallow any more.

The men leave. Are we going now? They signal for me to follow them. We follow a narrow path into the valley, all in a line. I struggle to hobble along behind the locals, but I cannot keep up with them. Although they are all considerate and wait for me, I still lag far behind. Up ahead, they cross a stream onto a plateau. From afar the place looks like a fortress of sorts but it turns out to be a summer settlement, with huge boulders and wooden fences enclosing the small plateau. Slowly, I get closer and can see a few huts standing between a couple of big trees. Behind this, in a little meadow, little goats run about with an equal number of children. There is a donkey standing in the middle of the yard, braying.

After all this time on my own, I have finally come across somewhere I can stay! I felt safe now. There were children and animals everywhere and I could stay for some time. However, I am concerned that none of my team have come looking here and that my mother still does not know of Günther's death.

Nagaton

The woodcutters first speak at length with the men at the hut. They point in my direction several times, as I stand amongst the children looking lost and hopeless. They then lead me to a big tree. One of them lays out a cloth and I sit down, and then lie down using my bundle as a pillow. I take my outer boots off and place them next to me. My feet are so swollen by this stage that they no longer fit into normal shoes. Two women are standing between the huts.

The children get closer and are soon sitting round me in a circle. They watch as I massage my sorry feet. The women and girls standing in their doorways, glance over at us. One of the men then brings me a lassi, a yoghurt-like drink. I gulp down the whole tin-cup full and thank him. But do they understand me? They give me another piece of chapatti. I chew the bread carefully, trying to indicate that I am in need of liquid nourishment. 'Lassi?' I croak; my throat is so swollen. I try once more to describe my situation using sign language.

They shake their heads in disbelief. The name Nanga Parbat can be heard amongst their mutterings. I point to the other side of the mountains and, using my index and middle fingers, show a walker. 'Tap: Base-Camp?' I ask. More shaking of heads. One of them bursts out laughing.

No, they have not understood a thing. I want to know how far it is to the Tap Alpe base camp, how many days. 'Din?' I say and show two, three, four fingers?

'Din' means day. I know that from our Sherpas. How else does one find out about distances?

I need to know how many days. I try again, showing one, two, three and four fingers. They all look at me questioningly with curious expressions, but there are no confirmations or negations forthcoming. I place a stone on the ground again and trace the route with my finger.

'Nanga Parbat,' I explain.

All nod. Now I draw a little cross in the dirt with my index finger. 'This spot on the ground, next to the stone, is Tap Base Camp,' I explain once more.

All nod once more. So they have understood after all. I then draw another cross, exactly opposite the departure point, the other side of the stone, which is the mountain.

'Diamir' I say. 'This is where we are, in Diamir.'

They all nod. How far is it from Tap to Diamir?

I trace an arc between the two points all the way around the right of the mountain and ask the audience 'Din?' Their faces light up.

Two, is the figure one of them shows me; it should take two days. Another shakes his head and points to my feet.

What he means was that it would be two days but not with these feet. My frostbitten feet would not make such a tough journey. Impossible! And what about the trek down the valley from there? I had to make it to Rupal Base Camp or to Bunar, somehow! Again, I think of my mother. What is the date? As I look at my watch, I find it has stopped, on the 29th.

Today must be the first of July I think to myself. The others would have been here long ago if they were searching for us.

I wind up my watch with some difficulty. It has to be done with my left hand as my right hand is frostbitten. The alarm goes off. They all look on in amazement. A little boy nudges my elbow. He wants my watch. No, I still need it for a bit but I give it to an old man to hold. Fascinated, he loses himself in this wonder-world and plays with it. He is like a child with an electric train set. He wants to have it too; wants to buy it. I shake my head. No. I tell myself I will still need it. Maybe even to barter for food or as payment for the trip down to Gilgit.

By now, night has already fallen. A small fire is made. Nobody talks anymore. As I try to sleep, the stars illuminate the whole sky. The locals disappear, just like shadows, one by one, they slink off to their huts. All that is left is a pile of glowing embers.

For the fist time in weeks I sleep properly. Later on, the place comes alive. A hunched figure paws at my outstretched arm and nimble fingers try to take my watch off. I only sense this but act on it, suddenly pulling my hand away. The man runs away. I take my watch off, put it in my pocket and open my eyes. The Orion constellation is now partially visible.

I lie there, gazing up into the vast expanse of the night sky and the eternal void. The last few days' events keep floating through my consciousness, like nightmares. Everything is spinning and I am spinning with the stars. I cannot sleep any more.

I kept on thinking of Günther. He was there but he wasn't there. If only he were here next to me. Everything would be all right then.

Where was he now? When and where did I let my brother out of my sight? I did not know. Again and again, I tried to determine when it was that I began hallucinating. Where and when had I started to talk to myself? The cold and wind rattled some of my loose connections into line. But answers? No. All the answers were painful, the same kind of feeling that amputation brings on.

When I wake up again I am surrounded by people. I do not really know what they want. I can only make out their outlines, and dark shadows around them. The air is smoky. I sit upright and stay there for a bit, staring at my feet. The swelling has gone down a bit in the cool night air. Just then, I notice my socks are missing. Somebody must have taken them in the night. It is not the end of the world, I figure, I can get into my shoes easier without them. I put the inner boots on and with a pained expression, squeeze them into the outer boots. I wrap my pullover, angora underwear, a hat and a few bits and pieces in my anorak and hand it to a boy standing next to me. He immediately understands that this means I want him to come with me.

I let him know that he will get my gloves and a head torch in return. Okay? He seems happy. I then get up by means of a tree stump, using it as a prop. With faltering steps, I move outside into the dawn. Suddenly I lose my balance and nearly fall over, but manage to catch myself on the porter's arm and stand still. For a moment we both sway. Leaning on my companion, I take a few steps. I try to overcome the pain and then take a few steps on my own. With great care, I hobble forwards. The porter is one step ahead. We both stop. I notice that my ice axe is missing. I wave my hands about angrily and mime hacking away at a lump of ice. After a short while, somebody brings the ice axe to us. Now I have everything. We carry on, cross the stream by a little bridge and soon disappear into the woods. We are on our way to Diamir but are still in the upper valley. The young man walking ahead of me is carrying my bundle of clothes as well as the axe and is very patient, always waiting for me to catch up.

A short while later, two boys run past us, each carrying a bundle of wood on his back. When they see me, they stop. The smaller of the two, barely eight years old, sits down. I would guess his bundle weighs about 10kg. My companion also sits down but I stand, hunched over in the shade of a tree.

I carefully creep towards the others. Just as I am about to sit down, my porter stops me. He knows how difficult it is for me to get on my feet again. On we go! But I cannot carry on; I must

The upper Diamir Valley between Nagaton and Ser.

rest, cool my hot feet, and drink. I am so thirsty! And in constant pain.

The others chat with one another. Two women now come along the path wearing wide breeches, tied at the ankles. They give us a wide berth and overtake us. One of them is carrying a bucket of water. I am so thirsty I beg her for some; I mime drinking water, tilting my head back and raising a cupped hand to my mouth. The boys have understood and go to talk to the women. At first, they refuse. After a bit, they push forward a young girl holding a watering can, indicating that I should drink from that. The water in the can is milky and tastes of grit and ice.

I should probably not be drinking this water, I think to myself. There is a risk it might be infected. My thirst is overpowering though, and my throat a burning wound. The cool moisture feels good.

I drink for a long time, nod my thanks and return the can. The women continue on their way. Every now and again, they turn to look at me and laugh.

But I was not in the mood to laugh.

Further ahead, I see a village, maybe two dozen houses in all. Around it are alternating fields of maize and grazing land. The fields are cut into the hillside in terraces and I can also see a steep track leading to the village. I stand and watch to see if any Europeans are there.

'Diamir?' I ask my companion and I point to the houses with my walking stick. The porter nods. 'Ser' he says dryly and carries on.

Ser

I am now close to the huts, which are made of stone with flat roofs and wooden doors, with no windows. There is a steep path leading straight through the middle of the village. We come to a halt on a grassy patch of land where there is a roofed well with clear water. I drink first and then lower myself to the ground. I take off my boots once more and dunk my feet in the water. They have swelled into clubfeet and my toes are dark blue and blood seeps from the pores. An old man watches me and shakes his head in disbelief.

Several children, youths and men soon surround me. All of them look at me with great curiosity. Some of them look stunned, as if I had come from a different planet. I want to know if any foreigners have been past. 'Sahibs?' White men,

264

like me? All of them shake their heads. They gesture that no 'white man' has been past for several years now.

Amazed that none of our expedition has been here, I fear that by now they might already be on their way home. I have no money with me, no ticket, nothing. I have no ID, no passport, not even a map of the area.

In the meantime, the sun has lit up the valley basin. One of the boys next to me is grinding up some grain in a stone mortar. He grinds the whole kernels between two stones and then adds water, producing a pulp that looks like tar. Without warning, he smears the paste on my toes, which immediately start to burn. My feet now hurt so much that all I want to do is lie in the shade, at least for a little bit. Two boys help me to my feet and bring me to the open entrance of a hut only two paces away from the fountain. Yes, they gesture, I should go into the prayer house. It is cool in there.

I have to take my shoes off before going in. Once inside, I lie down on a bed of hay, which is spread out everywhere, and close my eyes. The dried grass on the floor feels like a carpet. I am spread-eagled on the floor, with no shoes and my eyes shut. I try to sleep but I cannot manage it. This dark room, only 4m by 4m, and barely 2m high is so nice and cool; and it is quiet, too. But I am still scared, of what I do not know.

In one corner of the room, there is a hole in the wall and I can see leaves reflecting the sunlight. Suddenly, the door swings open and I jump. A barefooted man with a grey beard walks in, a gun slung across his chest. He looks eerie in his traditional pale robes. I stay motionless in my corner. At first, the intruder stands still in the middle of the room. Then he begins to talk, softly, lifting his hands and spreading them out. He then crouches down, kneels and bends down to the ground, gets up again and raises his eyes to the ceiling, lifting his arms as if in prayer. His words are spoken slowly and clearly like a poem.

In Ser.

He barely notices me and leaves the prayer house as quietly as he arrived. A little later, the door opens again. This time two men come in, one of them carrying a gun. The older one of the two sits down in the opposite corner to me. He is big and strong, and his black moustache gives him the air of a devil. The other one sits next to me, his gun on his lap. Instinctively I grab for the ice axe lying next to me. Afraid, I look at the man sitting next to me and then at the other, who is now staring at me. The man with the gun is young, maybe twenty-five. His face is narrow and paler than the others here.

'You policeman?' I ask.

266

They say nothing. After a while, the man with the gun shakes his head. His cartridge belt, which he has slung across his torso, also has a powerful effect on me. The other guy smirks.

I remember stories of people who had disappeared in this area: trekkers, scientists and tourists. They had simply vanished. Most of them were Europeans. Perhaps they were murdered somewhere in the mountains by the Chilas people.

I get up, feel my way along the wall and step outside. I suddenly feel a dizzy spell coming on and have to lean against the wall for support. Since I can no longer stand, I crouch down.

Later, I crawl to the edge of the path. There are children playing or just sitting there. People stand around me and again I begin to communicate with the villagers in sign language. I must let them know that I need someone to help me. I promise them bits of gear in return – that is all I have. A few seem to understand. One of them even picks up the yellow nylon overtrousers lying next to me but then puts them down again. Not enough perhaps? I can't work out what he wants.

'Eggs?' I ask, after a while. They all look at me in amazement. Apparently nobody understands. So I imitate the sound of a chicken and with thumbs and fingers, trace the shape of an egg for them.

The one with the overtrousers looks at me questioningly. I indicate five and act as if eating them. One of them nods. Apparently he has understood me. 'Eggs, chapatti and chai,' I repeat.

The overtrousers man runs off. How can I tempt any helpers though? I offer everything I can manage without. They do not understand. So I divide the remainder of my gear into three piles. One of the men points to my shirt however. No, I say, it is my last one. They can have everything else. Why do they have to have my last shirt, of all things? The lads talk to each other and arrange things. Are we in agreement?

In the meantime, a little boy has brought a pan. Another brings some wood. I sit there and clear everything out of their way. The overtrousers man now arrives with a burning piece of kindling and lights the fire. When I explain that we also need butter and salt they understand better. They place the flat pan on its three legs, directly on the fire. I put some butter in the pan and start cracking the eggs that the overtrousers man hands me, one by one. Next to me, another of them grinds some salt on a stone and starts to sprinkle it onto the fried eggs. Yet another brings some oven-fresh chapattis and a mug full of tea. They even bring me a spoon. It is from a previous Nanga Parbat expedition. My first real meal in over a week is now ready.

Whilst eating, I try to entice the young men into helping me. Surely one of them will want to help. Anything I offer is too little, however. One after the other, they all disappear.

I have had a lot of experience with foreign people; people whose language I do not speak and whose area I do not know. I have traded with them and eaten with them. Many of them were helpful, all of them were welcoming and I believe in human kindness. I was now relying on these foreigners. I was dependent on their bread, their shelter and their help. For the first time in my life, I was utterly at the mercy of the locals. I was so helpless. I could not even walk any more. And they knew it, and made sure that I knew that they knew. For the first time ever, I was placing myself in the hands of strange people in a real emergency situation. It was a chance to test my faith in human nature.

There are only two boys left with me now, and a few children. The two adults indicate that they want to help me. In exchange, they want all my gear. 'Yes,' I say and nod encouragingly. When they point at my shirt again, however, the shirt off my back, I can no longer contain myself and get angry. I point to my battered feet. They bring me my inner boots. They are still too tight. I look around for my outer boots. They seem to have vanished. The locals stand around, looking at me warily. Have they stolen them? I finally explode with such violent anger that the boys start. 'I want the boots! What have you done with my boots! The boots!'

One of them disappears behind the prayer house and returns with the heavy leather boots. I put them on, without the inner boots. I then wrap my anorak round my waist. I feel like a hunted animal, about to encounter his hunter down a narrow track.

I make my decision. I am going to go it alone. As absurd as it may sound, I have to make my way downward. Many miles from the next village and with severe frostbite, I was determined to keep fighting as long as I had the strength to. Would I make it all the way to the Indus Valley?

My feet are now so swollen that they are like clumps of wood in my boots, the pain throbbing like a ticking clock. How many hours would I last until I died?

With my ice axe in my left hand and a stick in my right serving as a crutch, I wobble my way through the village. I am almost on all fours, like an animal at death's door. All I can make are tiny, stiff steps forwards. Dilapidated huts lie to my left and right, and dirty little children watch me as I crawl past. Chickens lying in the dirt take a few steps to get out of my way. A woman standing in her doorway retreats in to the shadows as I pass her. One or other of my knees gives way every now and again and my whole body wobbles when one of my shoes hits a stone.

The path begins along a slope; the ground drops away steeply at the edge of the village. A fall here would be deadly for me. I look around.

Once again, I feel as if I have been here before, as if I am experiencing everything simultaneously. There is no past, no future, just the present. I am walking into the hangman's noose.

I cover the last few metres across the green swathe hesitantly and then stop and stare down into the steep, rocky gully. A river rages way below. Further down, the valley looks impassable. Nearby, two men are watering a cornfield

The Diamir river below Ser.

no larger than a sitting room by diverting the blue glacial waters through small irrigation channels in the ground.

That is how we used to play with water as kids, I think to myself.

Hesitantly, I ask for directions. One of them points down to the river, the other shakes his head. Is he trying to warn me? Trying to tell me that the Diamir is impassable on foot? That I will never make it my condition?

Murderer or Saviour?

Uncertain now, I stand at the edge of the village. Where to? I wonder, and look back. Way above, the Nanga glaciers are glistening. Two men come up to me now; once again, one of them has a gun! They try to tell me they want to come with me. Why, I'd like to know. To help me? The one with the gun was in the prayer house.

The gun makes me nervous. I can barely walk, let alone run away. What the hell, I have nothing left to lose, except my life of course, and I would somehow like to haul this threadbare life of mine home. Dreadfully tired now, I sit down. The guys sit down next to me, as if they too have nothing better to do. There is so much peace and tranquillity in this remote place.

There is no doubt that the Diamir gorge would be a perfect place to kill me in, unnoticed. My body would never be found. But would my mother ever find out what really happened if I disappeared?

I grumpily tell the guys they should head back to the village, but they insist on staying and show me they want to carry me. Only on the condition they leave the gun behind, I explain, using my hands and feet. They hand me the gun and I inspect it. It is English, perhaps from the Second World War and is not loaded. They both laugh and shake their heads. Their behaviour is genuine. I am embarrassed. What should I do? What next?

More to the point, what are my options?

I am exhausted and am getting slower and slower: tiredness and frostbite cripple my movements; everything hurts.

Suddenly, the guys take control of the situation. The unarmed one simply lifts me onto his back and off we go. Everthing seems to happen so fast. My carrier is either at a standstill or running. On difficult stretches, we all fend for ourselves, me on all fours, one of them in front and the other behind me. We get to a bridge made of two tree trunks with a couple of stone slabs resting on top, the river raging below, and I hesitate. One of the lads is already on the other side. Hunched over, I balance on top of the logs like a lunatic. I sway with every step. I hang motionless for a moment over the grey waters, then straighten up and carry on, like a drunkard.

It is changeover time when I reach the other side. The other lad hands his friend the firearm, cartridge belt and bundle of things, bends down backwards in front of me to let me sit up and hold onto his shoulders. He stands up and off we go down the valley.

Taking it in turns to carry me, they make their way down the valley. When we come across steeper slopes, I go it alone, either on foot or by crawling. We rest wherever we find shade. No, it would seem that my companions are not murderers, they are my saviours. I am grateful to them. My helpers also make up for my infirmity by giving me water, supporting me, reassuring me and keeping death at bay.

We stop at a hut and a farmer comes out and invites us in for a rest. I am instructed to lie down and stretch out on the plank bed in front of the door. One of the lads brings me some hot tea and the other two drink milk. For a while, the farmer studies me. Initially uncertain, he then sits by me and starts to massage my legs. Starting with my thighs, he kneads them, strokes them and presses them. What a lovely feeling. What agony! He works his way all the way down to my toes. After an hour of massaging, I indicate that we must push on down to Diamiroi. My two helpers have understood but are hesitant. Maybe they want to stay here for the night.

How many days had it now been since I became separated from the rest of the expedition? Every day counted! I was concerned about my frostbite and also about those at Base Camp. It was only natural to worry about them too. Herrligkoffer had no idea where I was and I felt bad about that. He had not heard any news from us for a whole week, so I had to move on. 'Get some help if I am too heavy but we cannot stay here,' I urge them.

I send one of the porters to Diamiroi to organize help and meet us en route. I then ask the lads from the hut to accompany the masseur and me down the valley. He should carry me on the flat terrain and then turn back once we are half way.

Karim, who fetched help from Diamiroi.

We split up. One boy runs ahead, the other stays with me and the masseur carries me. We take a narrow path, leading straight through the middle of the left-hand cliff faces of the gully, and follow the path, 300m above the river, along the steep cliff-strewn slopes. The sun is shining directly down on us and there is no wind whatsoever. Water? None. My throat, the fear, everything has dried out now. Just cliffs! Sheer vertical cliffs! The water rumbles by, way below. It rises in towers of froth, breaks and bubbles on its way. We crawl along between heaven and hell, scrambling here and there, and stare down into the depths where all we can see are vertical deserts of rock. Please don't slip anyone! The boys are wearing worn out leather shoes or are simply barefoot but are so nimble. I am amazed at how they can climb and still carry me.

273

Meanwhile, in Diamiroi, some men stand around under the apricot trees in a dusty square. They have just finished work and are getting ready to help a sick sahib they do not even know. They have heard about him and want to go to meet him.

So they set off to meet us half way. They follow a route over rows of cliffs and slabs of rock. The three of us are now sitting on a ledge, resting. I rest my head on my knees and try to snooze while the others roast the needles of a shrub. Tobacco perhaps? A little boy suddenly appears from nowhere. He has come from down the valley and is on his way from Diamiroi to Ser. Has he seen anyone, I ask, and point towards Diamiroi. No, he shakes his head. Had we missed our helpers? Or does he not understand me?

I did not know then that it was impossible to miss each other on that path. There is only one route through the Diamir Valley and it is so narrow that going the wrong way is highly improbable. All I knew was that I did not have long to live.

Slowly, I drag myself up a steep gully, one helper in front and another behind. Occasionally, the guy in front gives me his hand to pull me forward, while the one behind makes sure I do not slide backwards. Every time, I believe this must be the last uphill section and every time, another one appears.

Meanwhile, a group of men and boys make their way up the narrow path of the Diamir gorge. There are even some children with them. They stop when they see us and wait for us to get down to where they are. Could it be that one of them is carrying a sick man on his back? The second one has a gun and what looks like a small bundle. A few words are spoken and then all of them head down together. We stop to rest again in the shade of a rock. There is a watering hole directly next to our resting place and, one after the other, my helpers cup their hands and drink. Just one of the boys uses his shirt as a filter and slurps the water through the material. I am thirsty too. Inch by inch I feel my way towards the

What the men from the Diamir Valley wear on their feet.

trough, on my hands and knees. The others help me. I lie there, breathing heavily and drinking, like an animal. They all stare at my face; it is sunburnt, scabby and dirty. My hair is tangled and bleached and I am caked in dried sweat and dirt and stare blankly into the distance. I signal that we must carry on. At least it means I am still able to think, even though I no longer have the energy to hope.

I was even scared while being carried now. A fall now would still be fatal and it was my duty to go home and help my mother understand what happened as well as explain things to the expedition leader. So I had to carry on, as quickly as possible. I had to make sure I did not die here.

Even the farmers can see that I do not have long to live and they carry me further. As I try to stop, they shake their heads as if to say, 'It's easy really. We'll manage.'

Suddenly they stop. The gorge is now finished and the valley opens out. Through the leaves of a tree I can make out some fruit trees. Apricots! They point them out to me and one of the boys throws stones at the branches. They collect the ones that have fallen and bring them to me. It is the first fresh fruit I have eaten in two months!

The men take turns carrying me like a sack, all the way to the village. I sit slumped on their backs and look at the countryside. Irrigation channels stretch across meadows and fields.

It is the same now as it was in the stone age. I am amazed at how antiquated this world seems. The locals only go down to the Indus Valley or Gilgit once in a lifetime, with a handful maybe going more frequently. They live the self-sufficient existence of a bygone age.

Diamiroi

Our procession comes to a halt in the square at Diamiroi, a dusty space between a couple of stalls and huts. I am at a loss at first, then someone brings me a rudimentary stretcher so that I can lie down. There are children, men and youths standing around me. A short while later, someone brings tea. Now they all want to know where I have come from. Again, I take a stone and trace out my route, just like I had shown the woodcutters, although this time it is more thorough because I am practised at it now and I have also learnt a few words of Urdu, the local language. I then lie down and try to get some sleep.

My stretcher is a four-legged structure with leather straps woven into a net across the top. I feel like a fakir. I am so thin now that everything hurts, so I lie down on the ground next to the 'bed', put my windproof jacket under my head and sleep. Not for long though. I am suffering from dysentery and repeatedly have to drag myself away from my resting place.

276

In the early morning, a couple of men help me to my feet. I try to take a couple of steps but my feet refuse to support my weight and I fall down. The men are prepared to carry me further on their backs, the way they had done yesterday, but this method of transport hurts so much that I have to get down. 'We cannot do it this way,' I tell them.

Meanwhile, on the other side of the mountain at Rupal Base Camp, preparations were being made for the journey home. They were celebrating and working hard at packing up with crates lying around everywhere, as if they were soon to leave. The expedition leader was handing out medals to the Sherpa team. It looked like an athletics meet. Herrligkoffer: 'The Sherpas will be given gold, silver and bronze medals to recognize the effort they made. According to the country's custom, our liaison officer will present wreaths to Felix Kuen and Peter Scholz. These have been made for the summiteers by the high-altitude Sherpas.'

I do not have a clue that these events are occurring. I am not expecting any help from the Rupal Valley either though, not any more. Instead, I try to arrange my onward transportation from Diamiroi.

My whole body is in pain. The pressure I feel on my chest, which was already unbearable yesterday, is still with me today – I had spent ten whole hours on the back of a porter after all. I really cannot bear to be carried this way anymore. My helpers are at a complete loss and leave me there.

Did they want to see if I could manage it alone?

There is no way that I can walk. I sit down and communicate to them that they should make me a stretcher somehow, but the men do not understand what I want. So I ask them to bring two wooden poles, each of about two metres. I need two more; shorter ones this time. I place them across the two long ones at one and a half metre intervals. I pull a thin rope out of my pocket and bind the short poles to the long poles. They bring me some yak-hair rope and I weave a net between the poles. An hour later, the stretcher is finished. I place another anorak on one of the cross bars and manoeuvre my crippled body onto it, turning onto my back. Four men pick the stretcher up and another two then take it over. The whole thing sways and I very nearly fall off. They want to strap me onto the stretcher. No way! I shake my head. I am loath to lose the last bit of freedom of movement I still have.

I end up with six lads accompanying me. There are two men carrying the stretcher at any one time, while the other four follow behind and recuperate. They handle the contraption with skill, even when crossing a river. The porters have trouble keeping their balance but manage to reach the left bank and work their way further downstream. The path crosses a steep scree slope. Far below the path, the Bunar River flows by, taking huge boulders with it in its brown meltwaters as it thunders past. They will get me through this, I think to myself. The masses of rocks in the Bunar Valley are very worrying, however, and the path is as narrow as a thread as it crosses the slopes. It is the only path home and there is no drinking water in sight.

By midday, we make it to the Bunar Bridge over the Indus. The heat has put me in a trance and my hunger is now unbearable. But there are no houses, nor any green to be seen anywhere, just sand, rocks and inhospitable surroundings. The sand has tainted the colour of the river. I had to find some shade somewhere and drink, drink, drink. Once again I was close to delirium. I was also impatient. I could not miss the others. If they left without me I would not even be able to prove my identity, let alone anything else. And I was in a very foreign country too.

Herrligkoffer and the team were now on their way to the Indus Valley and Gilgit. Their journey home had now begun. There was no way that I could have known it but at the same time, a jeep convoy was setting off from the east of Nanga Parbat down the Astor Valley. Base Camp had been struck. Our expedition was heading home.

278

In the Indus Valley

There are a couple of people lying under the Bunar Bridge, gesticulating frantically to each other, unable to hear above the deafening sound of the river. The meltwaters are raging past on their way from Nanga Parbat. I lie on a concrete slab and gaze in the direction of the Indus. There seems to be a dirt road from here to the Indus, which looks like it is passable with a vehicle. The stretcher is leaning up against a rock on the side of the road. There is an old rusty, beaten-up tin can full of water beside me. The water from the Bunar River is dirty but I still drink it.

Do motor vehicles really come past here? If so, then when? I ask myself. I found it impossible to think clearly. This waiting was torture. Time has never passed so slowly.

Suddenly a jeep comes round the corner and disappears again in a cloud of smoke. It is heading south, in the opposite direction to me. I am disappointed but at least I now have a glimmer of hope. I do not feel quite as lost as I did. There really are vehicles here.

'The car,' I signal to the people, 'Where has it gone?' I would need a Jeep or some other similar form of vehicle. A Jeep would be ideal. If only a Jeep would appear.

Suddenly, the sound of a motor engine can be heard. Finally! The porters jump to their feet. It's a Jeep! And it is heading in the right direction, towards Gilgit. The porters run out into the road waving their arms and shouting. The vehicle comes to a halt and two military men get out. They listen to the porters and then signal for me to come over. I am carried onto the road. The two men from the Jeep, much larger in close-up, study me carefully. One of them seems to be an officer. They are sceptical at first. I do not exactly look good! They are still quite curious though.

'Where are you coming from?' asks one of them.

'Nanga Parbat – Tap Alpe – Base Camp Rupal Face,' I say, and show them the ascent route with my right hand. 'Diamir' I say, and point again.

The officer shakes his head incomprehendingly.

'Top, descent on the Diamir side,' I explain further.

Once again, the officer shakes his head. It was as though he wanted to say that is impossible. I am nevertheless told to get in and the driver pulls away. My helpers wave me off. I could only give them what was left of my equipment.

'Pictures?' he asks.

He has now turned around and is looking at me questioningly. I pull a Minox camera out of my pocket and show it to the officer. He has definitely not seen anything like it before. He holds it in his hand and pretends to take photos. 'James Bond?' he asks.

He is studying me again.

I wonder what people must think of a person who appears out of nowhere, half dead. I am sure that, for a while, the officer takes me for a spy or a criminal of some kind.

'No, no, I am a climber, coming from Nanga Parbat.'

I am now sitting in the back seat of a jeep with a soldier next to me. He keeps his distance, as if he does not want to come into contact with such a foreign species.

I cannot bear to think what I look like and how I must smell.

The countryside is flying past: barren slopes, the Indus way below and, to the right of the road, vertical cliffs. On the other side of the river, there is the occasional village. When we reach a side valley, the driver turns off the road, drives to the end of the track and stops in front of some barracks. The officer gets out and talks to the guard. Other officers appear as well as a few soldiers.

'This person' is the only thing I understand, as they all swing their heads round to look at me sitting in the Jeep. Again and again I hear 'this person'. After a few minutes we move on. I have no idea where to, though. We are heading north, in

The four lads from the Diamir Valley who carried Reinhold Messner.

any case. Then I see a marker stone by the side of the road. I can see 'Gilgit' but cannot read the number next to it.

Our Jeep comes to a halt in a lay-by to let a truck get past. The high-top truck is brightly decorated like all Pakistani trucks, with little painted squares that tell a story. What story, I will never find out.

Hours later, when we finally pull up for the day, I am happy to get out. We are at the officer's apartment. He goes straight into the house and signals for me to wait outside. A little while later, somebody brings me a stool. I am to sit down. A servant then brings me something to drink. I thank him and tentatively ask if I may wash myself. Of course I can, he says, and leads me to the toilet.

Can that really be me? Looking in the mirror, I hardly recognize myself. I look so old and grey! The officer however, is a whole lot friendlier after I have had a wash.

He now serves up tea, cheese, potatoes and salad. His two exceptionally beautiful daughters sit down next to me and attempt to make conversation with me in broken English. The officer takes some photos. His wife is summoned. She joins us and I thank her for her hospitality. The lady smiles warmly. She and the two girls then go back into the house. Some other officers bring a map and ask me to show them where I have been. I trace the route with my finger; the route, which now only holds memories of hopelessness, despair and sadness for me. I cannot say anything about it though. After all, what language would I use? I only point out places, like 'Rupal; Base Camp; Nanga Parbat; Diamir; Diamiroi; Bunar; Jeep'.

They all stare at me in amazement, as if I have come back from the future or am from some mystical Shangri La. How can one man just walk over the mountain?

I do not reply. I still have to work out myself how I managed to survive the whole dreadful odyssey. What incredible luck I have had. It is verging on a miracle and impossible to explain; for now, in any case. The questioning faces now looking at me stir up some doubts in me, doubts about my own experience and my own memories. Was it my own life that I had saved in the Diamir Valley or did it belong to someone else?

Suddenly I am surrounded by school children, all dressed in white, there to inspect the invalid. They help me into the

Jeep. Farewell and many thanks. A wave. The officer stays there with his family but has a quick word with the driver before we set off. He instructs that I am to be taken to Gilgit as fast as possible.

The only words I understand are 'hospital' and 'Gilgit' but they are enough to reassure me. They have understood my wishes. I am touched by their willingness to help.

'Well, you say, you are coming from Nanga Parbat?' asks the driver, after a while.

'Yes,' I reply.

'Strange. How can it be possible? Your Base Camp – isn't it on the other side of the mountain?'

'Yes. But I came down the Diamir side.'

'I heard on the radio that two man died there.'

'I am one of them.'

There was no way I could explain everything to him there and then as we drove along. My English was not good enough in those days and he had to keep his eyes on the road. Somehow, I was born again. Was this my second life?

The drive is one long struggle. I am sitting in the back seat, holding tight to the front seat. Every bump in the road gives me a jolt. Again and again I am thrown out of my seat.

We have crossed the Rakhiot Bridge already. How much further is it? I carefully study the road signs. Another 40 miles to Gilgit. Thirty-two; twenty-eight; twenty-five.

A policeman stops us along the way. They salute each other and the driver explains something to him. Apparently he explains what his orders are. They talk for a short while and the Jeep takes off again in a cloud of dust. Just 20 miles to Gilgit now.

The ground falls away steeply on one side of the dirt road and the mountains rise just as steeply on the other. The road has been cut out of a cliff. The Jeep stops again. Huge boulders lie in the the road, some of them are right in the middle of the road, blocking our way.

The driver gets out and walks up to the barrier, where he speaks to a soldier. I lie on the back seat, somewhat perturbed. I still cannot quite tell what is wrong. The driver comes back and gives me something to drink.

He then turns the Jeep around. We have to go back one mile and go down a side road. What's going on? We stop at the first settlement to make a phone call. I am told to get out. 'Wait here,' the driver says.

Night has now fallen. I am lying absent-mindedly on a stretcher bed in front of one of the huts. I can hear the sound of pressurized drills. Will the road soon be open? I am incredibly grateful to these soldiers. They are doing all they can to help me get to the nearest hospital as fast as possible. A few men in uniform are standing around me. I ask them if they too have heard that two men went missing on the Nanga Parbat expedition. No. Why? I would have thought it was common knowledge. Herrligkoffer would surely have reported that two of his team were gone, missing for days already. But who reads newspapers? And there is no search party underway.

I could not understand why my rescuers, the farmers and the officers had heard nothing whatsoever about a search operation; nothing about the fact that Günther and I had disappeared; nothing about an actual search. A notice had not even been posted in the local paper about our tragedy. Maybe Herrligkoffer was waiting until there really was no more hope. He either believed he would see us again or he believed in miracles. It did not make sense. Surely one could not post a missing persons' notice without actually sending out a search party to look for them.

284

Chapter XIII

The Summit Triumph

The Diamir Face.

What still remains a mystery is why the two men decided to go down an unfamiliar route into unknown territory on the Diamir Face. There were no camps set up, no fixed ropes and no help to be had. It makes no sense whatsoever. And it was exactly there, on the Diamir Face, that Günther lost his life.

Karl Maria Herrligkoffer

Peter Scholz, Max von Kienlin and Felix Kuen.

There were only 6m left to go and I finally stood on the summit of the long-desired objective, the cursed yet beloved Nanga Parbat.

Felix Kuen

I came across a clump of felt, kicked it in front of me and had no idea that it could possibly have been Reinhold Messner's frozen gloves, which he later maintained he had left for the Himalaya gods as proof of his ascent.

Felix Kuen

Way up, on the highest point, I rammed my ice axe into the mass of the mountain. The flags of Pakistan and Tyrol, which were attached to it, fluttered in the wind.

Felix Kuen

Triumph and Tragedy

Flashback: Felix Kuen and Peter Scholz stood on top of the 8125m peak of Nanga Parbat, one day after we had. On their way up they had heard some cries for help and in the late hours of that morning had briefly been in radio contact with me. They reported this, upon their return to camp 4 together with the fact that they had found a piece of felt.

Just like us, Felix Kuen had apparently suffered from hallucinations on his way down, due to exhaustion and a lack of oxygen.

Kuen: 'I was often in a state of trance through the lower section of the Merkl Couloir. I suddenly saw hundreds of little men climbing up to Camp 5. They were Japanese. They wanted to pass us and storm the summit. Our summit! My summit! I called over to Peter Scholz: "The Japanese are coming! Do you see them?" "You're going mad!" said Peter, "You are crazy!"'

When Kuen and Scholz returned to Base Camp, they told the expedition leader how they had reached the summit and that they thought we must have gone down into the Diamir Valley.

'What foolishness! How irresponsible!' said Kuen.

Herrligkoffer: 'Descending by way of the Diamir Valley has absolutely nothing to do with our expedition's goals.'

The expedition leader was correct of course but we had no choice. Since we were not willing to die of cold, of dehydration and of lack of oxygen, we were forced to risk an unsecured descent route. The route was chosen out of despair and would lead to a desperately tragic conclusion. It was our only escape route, thrust upon us by an

Felix Kuen with the 'summit flag' at Base Camp.

unavoidable situation. It was I alone who carried the responsibility for it.

The conquest of the Nanga Parbat summit, which for Felix Kuen was the greatest triumph of his life, turned out to be the worst tragedy in my life. With a bit of luck I will survive this 'madness' and be saved.

In the meantime, Base Camp beneath the Rupal Face had been struck and the expedition team was on its way home. Did any of them believe they would see us again? Could Günther and I still be alive?

It was on this night, 20 miles outside Gilgit, that Karl and I crossed paths. It was by sheer chance, in the middle of the night.

I had already surrendered myself into the hands of fate. I knew then that I had survived thanks to a large helping of luck. I no longer had the strength to fight with the man,

288

anyway. All I wanted to do was to explain myself, explain what had happened and share my utter despair.

Reunion with Herrligkoffer

There was the sound of a motor engine in the night. A Jeep stopped and Karl and Alex got out. There were people standing around the stretcher on which I lay. Karl came closer and stopped a moment in front of the camp, which now looked like a sick bay. Finally, they had come! Herrligkoffer was confused. Hesitantly, he came closer and realized he recognized the patient. I was in a wretched state: my face was like that of a ghost, thin and drawn, my lips all cracked and my gums all dry and broken. My shirt and trousers were ripped and dirty, my feet were shoved into my inner boots without socks. At once shocked and moved, Karl bent over me and began to stroke me. Not one word was spoken.

At first, Karl was very careful with me. He was sensitive and not at all dismissive. Not how he usually was with me, in any case. I was surprised. I had never seen any sign of compassion in him. Did he know how I was suffering?

Karl walked around my bed, smiled, looked at me understandingly and repeatedly stroked my arm. He even ran his fingers through my hair. I asked Alex to pull off my inner boots. My feet were very swollen and red and my toes were black.

'It is good that you are here, Reinhold.' Karl reassured me.

'We had to...' I began to explain but was interrupted and faltered. The two medics had arrived to inspect the frostbite injuries. They nodded to one another.

'Don't you worry. That isn't important right now,' Karl said, trying to pacify me.

'Günther must have been swept away by an avalanche, way down at the bottom,' Is what I wanted to say.

'You must concentrate on yourself right now.' Karl said it like an order.

He then took my right hand and very carefully looked at my fingers. Even my fingertips were black where they had been frozen. They felt like they were made of wood but hurt less than my feet.

'And the other hand?'

I shook my head.

'Just concentrate on yourself,' repeated Karl 'just on yourself.'

It had been four days since Günter's disappearance, although for me he was still there. Since he was neither in front nor behind me, I imagined him to be next to me. For four whole days, I had waited in desperation for him and for some help to turn up. The loss of Günther and the pain I had endured had been too much for me to cope with on my own.

Finally, some of the rest of the team arrived. Not one of them asked what it had been like. I was meant to forget about Günther never coming back. It was no longer important, said Herrligkoffer, I must only think of me. Sure, those words were meant to reassure me, but I still did not quite understand.

I just wanted to share my hurt, tell them everything, to no longer have to deal with loss, despair and responsibility on my own. If the brother that had only days ago stood on the peak with me was now no longer there, how could I just suddenly forget that he was missing? How? The most important fact was not supposed to be important? No, I could not find comfort in that, nor could I sleep. I was perplexed.

Later on, I was laid down on the back of an open-top Jeep. A few porters sat next to me on rucksacks and crates, Alex and Karl sat in the cabin with the driver. That night, we reached Gilgit, and with it, civilization. I was finally able to see all of the people we had worked with for so many weeks, even Felix, who had often gazed at us enviously. Max was moved to tears.

290

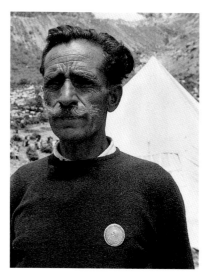

The sirdar Isar Khan.

Gerd, our liaison officer, and Jürgen were saddened. There was just one person who was not happy to see me back.

It is just a feeling I have but Felix had a pained expression on his face and was avoiding me. Why would he not talk to me?

Max came to visit me in hospital the next day. He was annoyed and excited at the same time. 'The red flare, do you remember it?' he asked.

I sat up in bed, looked straight ahead and tried to focus. My thoughts were miles away. 'It was such a long time ago,' I said 'but it is the only reason why I set off to the summit alone.'

'Yes, exactly – can't you remember the radio conversation: "I feel the same way" and so on?'

'I had not thought of it until now. The only thing that mattered was finding an alternative route down.'

'He set off the wrong flare!'

'A red one.'

'The weather forecast was good.'

'The weather forecast was good?' I asked in disbelief.

'Yes. That evening, on the radio, he gave us a good weather report. He should have shot off a blue flare.'

'That is what we agreed on; a red flare for bad weather and a blue one for fair weather. And you say the weather forecast was good? But the flare that was fired was red wasn't it?'

'Yes, exactly. We were all shocked to see a red flare go up when we had heard the weather report was good. Were you not surprised up there?'

'We were, for a moment.'

We were so far away, so high up, focused on ourselves. And once we had left Camp 5, the three of us, Gert, Günther and I, were solely responsible for ourselves. That's just how it was. As the eldest of the three, I adopted the role of spokesman and so took the lead. Günther followed me. Certainly I wavered for a second, but I was never really unsure. I knew what I had to do.

'Is that not what we had agreed upon?' I asked after a while. 'Can you remember?'

'Yes, I heard the conversation.'

'So, Max, why the red flare when the weather report was good?'

'He said he mixed them up.'

'Mixed up? Red instead of blue?'

'Did you not question it instantly?'

My whole life long, I have always trusted others; always analysed things but in the end always trusted them. And now I was suddenly meant to have questioned such an important message. The 'bad weather' flare was our signal to get off the mountain.

'He surely cannot claim that red flares look the same as blue flares. There must be a difference, mustn't there?'

'He said there was a blue seal around the red flare.'

'Around the red flare?'

'Yes, it was only as the flare went up that we could tell that it was red.'

'So why was a blue one not sent up straight afterwards?'

'He had no blue ones.'

'But when we talked over the radio at midday, he said that he had blue ones as well. Karl himself went to see what colours he could offer me. He told me he only had red or blue.'

'That is exactly right. Hermann and I heard it on the teleport machine. It was you, Felix, Günther, Peter and Gerd at Camp 4, and Werner, Gert and Hansi at Camp 2. At midday he said that he had blue flares and by the afternoon, there were suddenly none left. You do not make two mistakes in such an important matter. First the wrong flare and then not having a second one.'

Karl steered clear of me and we did not speak anymore. It was as if we existed in separate cocoons. We were like two hurt people, who could not open up to one another.

A few days later, we were flown to Rawalpindi in a Hercules helicopter. I gazed pensively out the window as tatters of cloud blew past. Way below, I could see the Indus. Far away, hidden by cloud at first, a big mountain came into view. Its contours, like mosaic tiles, slowly came together to make a clear shape, that of a huge mountain. It was bigger than any other in the surrounding area. It was Nanga Parbat.

It was the only peak that was still covered in cloud. Beneath it lay the Diamir Valley. An air steward walked down the aisle handing out boiled sweets. Nobody else on board was quite as transfixed with the view out of the window as I was. The others spoke, read newspapers and held conversations. I was curious and infinitely sad at the same time. I pressed my nose against the window and had a long look down onto the glacier below the Diamir Face. Who is that? Karl took a seat next to me. Unexpectedly. At once shocked and grateful, I looked at him. For a moment it seemed like he wanted to say something to me, that we could talk to each other. The two of us had both lost our brothers here on this mountain. We would surely be able to talk about our own personal tragedies.

When Günther, my brother, was alive, it sufficed to know that he simply existed. Even when I had waited for him, I

*took it for granted that he remained a part of me. Now that
he was no longer alive, I could not bear the fact that he was
not sitting right next to me. Suddenly, it was not just the seat
next to me that was empty but also my soul that had been
drained, the memories a mere patchwork. Our dream of
Nanga Parbat had been destroyed, even though we had
stood on the summit together.*

Like a distorted image, I saw my reflection in the window
and jumped. My eyes were glazed over. Then I saw Gunther's
face. I saw his eyes at Camp 3, on the summit and at our first
bivouac. Clouds flew past. Karl was sitting back in his own
seat, far away, alone. Not a trace of sorrow to be seen in that
broken man's face.

Were Karl and I so very different? Both of us had lost our
brothers on Nanga Parbat, both were loners. Why were we
unable to talk about it? Were we like two autistics, who had
similar experiences but different recollections? Now, with
the expedition over, we no longer had any common goals.
Herrligkoffer, that despiser of mankind, no longer needed
me. We had become complete strangers.

In Rawalpindi there was a letter waiting, addressed to
Günther. I opened it and read:

'My dear ice cavemen!

Firstly, our sincerest best wishes and congratulations on
this mean feat – whether you have reached the summit or
not!!! My dear Günther, that was the most interesting letter I
have ever received or ever will receive. (That includes all love
letters too.) Written at 6000m on the 8th of the May and
stamped on the 17th – you must have turned back then? I
never dreamt that I would ever receive a letter from a
Himalayan expedition. On top of that, one written at 6000m!
(How many gloves did you have to wear?) I am so proud to
be the recipient of such a letter and felt as excited as you when
I read it! Our sweet little Antje had to wait to be fed until I
had finished reading it! Will we have the pleasure of seeing

you this year in 'Villnöss'?! Or are you going to race up every summit down there? If you cannot succeed on that steep face, then I do not know who else is capable.

Your return flight must land in Frankfurt. Don't you dare not call us and come to visit! We'll give you both a right royal reception!

Anyway, all the very best for the further success of your trip and once again, many thanks for the lovely postcards and the letter.

We greatly look forward to seeing you both again and hearing more about your great adventure.

The best of luck and mountain blessings! Love, Heidi'

The letter was to us both, so I read it twice.

Three days later, I landed in Frankfurt but I did not want to visit our friends on my own. Besides which, I had to check into the clinic as quickly as possible because of my frostbite and I wanted to go straight to the Innsbruck University Hospital.

A few days later I was registered as Professor Flora's patient: University Hospital, Room 8, tenth floor, vascular department. I was given infusions to encourage vascular expansion. Next to me on the table were letters, condolence telegrams and messages of congratulations. It had become clear that amputations were inevitable; several toes were to be removed. The doctors did all they could.

Every day, I read stories in the local papers of false estimations, foolishness and stupidity. The accusations that Günther was too weak for a summit attempt were repeated. I was in despair. It was not as if Günther could say anything or defend himself.

My frostbitten fingertips and seven toes were black. They felt numb. I would lose them. I would no longer be able to climb, the way I had climbed before Nanga Parbat.

That was not really that important though. How would I be able to carry on living without being able to explain that things had not been as they had appeared in millions of newspapers? How was I meant to deal with the death of my brother and our descent, when others were reporting and judging our disaster without listening to me, without having been there themselves?

Herrligkoffer's official expedition report appeared in the *Bunte Illustrierte* magazine, and it focused largely on the shouted conversation between Felix Kuen and myself.

Kuen: 'I heard a shout for help in the 500m long Merkl Couloir. When I stood on the top of the ridge at 11 o'clock I could see Reinhard 80m above us and I asked him what had happened. He replied that they had called for help between 6 and 9 o'clock because Günther was suffering badly from altitude sickness and did not dare to go down the fixed ropes of the Merkl Couloir. Reinhold asked us for a rope. We had already deposited our spare rope at the resting spot above the ridge, however. I suggested that he wait for us to come back.'

Had Felix understood more than he later admitted to understanding?

Chapter XIV

Epilogue

Avalanche on the Diamir Face.

Soon after our return, a thick and increasingly impenetrable veil was drawn over the events on the Rupal Face. It seemed as if all who had been there were being persecuted by the curse of the mountain gods as an act of revenge for the fact that their spirit had taken them from the lowly plains of human life to the pure, unsullied heights of the peaks of far Kashmir. Today we know the reasons behind this and we know, too, that they cannot detract from the experience of battling up the highest mountain face on Earth to stand atop that giant of rock and ice that the local people call 'Diamir', the 'King of the Mountains'.

Karl Maria Herrligkoffer

*Gloves and an ice axe on the summit of
Nanga Parbat.*

I climbed the last steep slope to the summit and held
up the pennant on the ice axe in the wind. At that
moment there was nothing more important for us in
the world than that tiny platform of hard packed snow
and bizarre rock formations. We were standing on an
eight thousander – and I was not dreaming! We were
so happy.

Peter Scholz

The view down into the Rupal Valley is breathtaking.
Below us, the Face drops sheer for almost 5000m.
From here, Base Camp is not visible to the naked eye.

Felix Kuen

On the mountains over 7000m, the ascent and descent
were made by the same route as a matter of course,
with three exceptions: during the 1951 attempt to
traverse the Nanda Devi massif, the strong French
team of Duplat and Vignes went missing; in 1963 an
American Mount Everest expedition under Norman G.
Dyhrenfurth made a successful traverse of the 'Third
Pole' (WNW–SE); in 1970 the brothers Reinhold and
Günther Messner traversed Nanga Parbat (8125m)
from S to NW – up the 4500m-high Rupal Face and
down the Diamir Flank.

Günther Oskar Dyhrenfurth

Inconsistencies

It was not just the episode with the red rocket that I had explained to me piecemeal. How could I possibly have known up there on the summit headwall that the mountain forecast for the 27th of June had been good?

Herrligkoffer: 'In accordance with the weather report received, Michl Anderl fired off a rocket with a blue seal around it. We were not a little shocked to see a red signal flare rising into the sky.'

In the early morning of 27 June 1970 the expedition leader, contrary to his usual habits, was looking at the Face through the telescope. He must therefore have spotted me in the Merkl Couloir, if only for a few brief moments. He must therefore have reckoned that I was going for the summit.

Herrligkoffer: 'We are now convinced that the team from Camp 5 is either fixing the Couloir or making a push for the summit.'

Initially, that was all he could really establish from his position down at Base Camp. From the valley, it was impossible to view the Merkl Couloir in its entirety. Later, the mist came down and covered the summit area. The question is: what exactly did the expedition leader expect of us?

Herrligkoffer: 'We spent the rest of the 27th of June observing the region above the camp with concentrated attention but there was nothing more to be seen. We came to the conclusion that the Messners and Gerd Baur were heading up towards the summit.'

He went on: 'Thus, we were all the more surprised that evening suddenly to see a figure emerge from the tent at

Camp 5 and start descending to Camp 4. We awaited the next radio call with eager anticipation, when we would learn from the returning climber what had occurred during the last twenty-four hours at Camp 5.'

When one of the men at Camp 4 later informed them that Gerd Baur had descended alone from Camp 4, by all accounts there was great excitement at Base Camp. That was understandable; no one down there could have foreseen that the summit team would consist of only two climbers.

Herrligkoffer: 'Gerd Baur reported that Reinhold Messner had set off during the night to climb the Couloir and also that Günther had followed his brother early next morning.'

Kuen: I find Günther Messner's achievement extraordinary. As we later learned, he climbed the Merkl Couloir solo in just four hours. The exertion might possibly have laid the foundations for his subsequent swift physical decline.'

I certainly shared this sentiment; indeed, it would become the basis for discussions about the expedition at a later date.

There was a mixture of perplexity and hope in the team. It was two days later, when Kuen and Scholz returned from the summit, before further details became clear. Herrligkoffer quickly pieced together all the information they had and concluded that we would turn up on the left-hand, easier part of the Rupal Flank.

Why was it that no one seemed to want to comprehend that Günther and I had no choice but to descend the Diamir Face? Because I had survived the seemingly impossible? The situation into which we had manoeuvred ourselves had in the end left us with no other escape option than to descend directly down the Face into the Diamir Valley.

Herrligkoffer: 'On the way down from the summit to the South Shoulder, Günther voiced the opinion that descending the Merkl Couloir would be too difficult for him. From where he was standing, Reinhold could see that the climb down to the Gap at the end of the Merkl Couloir was straightforward. A quick look at a photograph of the Rupal

Face that he had with him seemed to confirm that from there it would be possible to regain the Couloir and call for help.'

In fact, it was only after calling for help that the self-rescue operation began.

Kuen: 'Reinhold bent to pick something up; from his movements it looked as if it was a heavy rucksack. Reinhold then disappeared from the ridge.'

Herrligkoffer: 'The Messner brothers' rucksacks had been left behind in the tent at Camp 5.'

Why was it later implied that I had planned to make a complete traverse of Nanga Parbat? The insinuation was that I had gambled with the life of my brother through pure ambition. And what was Felix Kuen hoping to achieve with his 'observations', observations that were either pure fabrication or the result of a grave misunderstanding? What was he trying to say?

Was he trying to suggest that I had carried Günther? Or was the implication that he had died at the Merkl Gap, that on the morning of 28th June he was already dead?

Karl Maria Herrligkoffer later presented me with a sheet of paper containing an outrageous explanation of events.

Herrligkoffer: 'Reinhold Messner admits that he planned the descent of the Diamir Face when he bivouacked on the Diamir side. It was in the early morning that his brother began to suffer from serious altitude sickness and the brothers shouted down the Merkl Couloir for help from 6 o'clock to 9 o'clock. His brother Günther died before the second rope could bring help.'

Such cynicism! It was now clear what Herrligkoffer wanted. Although he could not have come up with this false statement of events himself I was both hurt and bewildered at one and the same time. In fact, I was sick with rage. Did this mean I was to be deprived of the right to explain my version of events? How could Herrligkoffer distort the facts in such a way?

Were we to accept that a mere observer knew better than those who had been directly involved in what had happened in the summit area of Nanga Parbat?

It was then that I began finally to doubt Herrligkoffer's loyalty and integrity. And there were other unanswered questions, too. Why was it only the second summit team that had taken a Pakistani flag with them? And why had we – Gerd, Günther and I – not been initiated by Herrligkoffer into the ritual of hoisting the flag on the summit? Why?

Had there been some kind of foul play going on during our expedition, like in 1953? Prior to our sad reunion, my relationship with Herrligkoffer had not been the best, but it had been objective and down-to-earth. Thereafter he had tried to placate me, but he failed to answer my questions and even went so far as to call into question all my memories of the events. Now, our dialogue was abruptly terminated. I was not looking for recognition in his eyes; it was more a matter of the correct representation of the facts, based on my experience and my position. To be sure, we could have found answers together to all the unanswered questions and in so doing we might well have gained an understanding of each other's behaviour and attitude. However, Herrligkoffer insisted on his exclusive right to report events as he saw them and was not interested in a collaborative expedition report. He, and only he, would be the one to explain how the expedition had gone, even though he had never been to the high camps, let alone to the summit area. Perhaps he felt he had to play the master, although he had failed conspicuously to master the situation as it developed on the mountain. In acquiring the sole rights to the experiences of Merkl, Buhl and me, he probably saw himself as judge and jury in all matters relating to Nanga Parbat while at the same time placing himself above the whole thing.

Herrligkoffer again played the expedition members off against each other, just as he had done in 1953. In return for

302

Reinhold and Günther Messner.

the promise that they would be allowed to participate in his next expedition – to Mount Everest – some of the team were prepared to endorse his version of events. In Herrligkoffer's expedition report the individual team members were classified good or bad according to whether they supported him in public debate or not.

At the time, climbing the highest mountain in the world was of no interest to me and I returned to the university, intent on pursuing a normal life. As an invalid with amputated toes I could see no future for me as a mountaineer.

My climbing career was over. Herrligkoffer had advised me immediately after our first meeting in Gilgit to give up mountaineering.

For many long months I lay in my bed in Room 8 on the tenth floor of the Innsbruck Hospital. I had many visitors.

Some came out of curiosity, others came out of sympathy. Most came for honest reasons but even they told my story wrong, just as they had read it in the newspapers.

Anyone who had been on this expedition himself could only marvel at how the same events could later come to be represented in such a contradictory way. New versions of the ascent of the Rupal Face kept cropping up as, with few exceptions, the expedition members went their own separate ways and gradually lost touch with each other.

Now, of course, it is too late for questions, even the question 'Why?' Why did Günther follow me up the route? Why was he ever on the trip? Why had nobody warned us?

Well, they had warned us. They had warned us about Herrligkoffer. But without him we would never have even set eyes on the Rupal Face and back then the challenge of the Rupal Face was stronger than all the warnings and all the doubts together. What an objective it was! It was, in a word, our dream. There was no mountaineering challenge that came close. Yes, Günther and I wanted to climb that face, or at least attempt it. And Herrligkoffer alone held the keys. He had the permission, the know how and the finance required. He alone could give us our chance.

When my parents visited me in hospital my father, too, was reproachful. Where is Günther?

He wanted to know. Yet before we set off it had been he more than anyone who had insisted that I make the case for Günther and push for his inclusion in the team.

My mother, of course, defended me. As for Herrligkoffer and I, our stances drifted further and further apart; so far, in fact, that it must have seemed as if two men who shared the same obsession were standing for opposing ideals. One and the same mountain of destiny – but no shared experience; one goal – but no shared values. We were not adversaries; we simply followed contradictory ideals of how life should be. We stood up for what we believed. And above us both stood the Naked Mountain.

Chapter XV

Mountain of Destiny

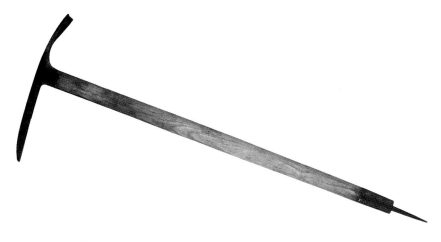

Hermann Buhl's ice axe.

Nowadays when I look at Reinhold Messner's
expedition style, I see that everything that Hermann
Buhl started decades ago on Nanga Parbat and
continued shortly before his death on Broad Peak – his
second eight-thousander – is indeed possible.

Eugenie Buhl

When talk turns to comradeship amongst mountaineers, the lowly plains dweller commonly maintains an awestruck silence. From what one learns about it in books and reports it seems to be the noblest of ideals, particularly so when applied to an expedition on which each is totally dependent on the others. Here, concepts like 'teamwork' and 'partnership' take on a completely different meaning. These young men, who travel to the Himalayas to scale the highest wrinkles on Earth, are the object of admiration and, possibly, incomprehension. They risk life and limb for something that is entirely useless. Nowadays that is in itself highly unusual. To be sure, since all of the 8000m peaks have now been climbed, some of them several times, public interest has diminished. Unless of course something 'happens'; for example, when cracks appear in the veneer of comradeship and the climbers, once home, turn out not to be the supermen they are occasionally considered to be, but individuals with their own weaknesses and character traits.

Süddeutsche Zeitung

The first ascent of the Rupal Face is a worthy counterpart to Hermann Buhl's world famous solo first ascent of the 'German mountain of destiny' in 1953. Unfortunately, the splendid achievement of the two South Tyrol climbers was tragically overshadowed by Günther's death in an avalanche.

Günther Oskar Dyhrenfurth

Günther's Climbing Journals

Learning to live with the loss of my brother, assuming responsibility for his death and coming to view my own survival as a rebirth, was a slow and painful process.

Herrligkoffer: 'It should not be my task to examine whether and to what extent Reinhold Messner was to blame for the death of his brother. When I found him again in the Gilgit Valley he was under great emotional strain and he will carry this burden to the end of his days. Neither is it my job to investigate whether he sacrificed his brother for his own mountaineering ambitions.'

I have now learned to live with such accusations and Günther's presence has helped me in this.

There was a time when I used to leaf through Günther's climbing journal only very occasionally. Now I find myself reading it over and over again.

1956: my first ski tours.

He was barely ten years old.

Furchetta with father and Reinhold.

Some German climbers gave us a rope. Previously, only our father had one.

Grosse Fermeda South Face.

We were still attending middle school when we did our first independent climbs.

1961 – Sass Rigais North Face – 800m – IV – difficult route finding; stonefall danger.

His first really big route. We were so proud of ourselves, particularly so since our father had failed on the route in his

307

youth and we now felt we had outgrown him.

Back then, we had only one climbing helmet and we took it in turns to wear it. Years later Günther soloed this route in two hours.

His first new routes.

He did them before his final exams at school.

Ortler North Face. Directly up the middle hanging glacier. First ascent of a very difficult variation.

From the outset he had always been particularly skilful on the ice.

Pelmo North Face in a dreadful storm.

It had been too late to abseil off.

Les Courtes North Face in four hours.

His first route in the Western Alps.

Triolet North Face – Lachenal Route – fourth ascent.

The fact that we only took three hours is down to him. He carried the rucksack. During the descent we did a new route on the west side of the North Face.

Badile North-East Ridge in a storm. Party stuck on the ridge. Solo climber went up past them to the top and they then descended together.

Günther went to the summit.

Langkofel North Ridge in one hour and fifteen minutes.

Günther was the only person I knew who could do this.

Hundreds of classic routes in the Dolomites.

I did not know it was so many.

Agnér, North-East Face direct: 1400m of steep rock climbing. One of the finest lines in the Dolomites.

I was proud of my brother.

Westliche Zinne: 'Scoiattoli Arete'.

Climbing with aids was not usually to his taste.

Marmolada di Rocca South Face – Vinatzer Route.

He climbed it twice.

Eiger North Buttress, first ascent, with Toni Hiebeler and Fritz Maschke.

Günther was in the best shape of all of them.

Retreat from the North Face of the Droites.

He was careful; he always had both feet firmly on the ground.

In the winter he preferred skiing to climbing. But who carried the rucksack for me on my winter ascents?

He did.

Five hundred routes and no falls.

Not many other people could claim that.

Aiguille d'Argentière – North-East Face; Central Pillar on the Heiligkreuzkofel; Grosse Fermeda – direct North Face; Cima della Madonna – North Face; a dozen new routes in the Geislerspitzen.

First ascents in the Eastern and Western Alps.

Second Sella Tower – direct North Face.

Few climbs compare for elegance and beauty.

'Now that first ascent was right up my street', he commented on the summit.

Between times, final exams at school (Abitur).

They went smoothly. No one expected anything else.

Spitz delle Roé di Ciampiedé – South Arete; Rocchetta – North Face and North-West Arete; Heiligkreuzkofel – Livanos Buttress; Kleine Zinne – Egger Route; Vertain – North Face via the hanging glacier; Presanella – North Face …

First ascents and early repeats of feared routes were our objectives at the time.

Gletscherhorn – North Face and Ebnefluh – North Face in a day.

He was the only person you could do things like that with.

Pelmo – North Face in winter: retreat from the top ledge system due to bad weather.

That was in December 1969. There were no more entries in his journal.

The next pages are blank. Photos, letters and sketches lie loosely between the pages.

It looked like he had been interrupted while sorting them all out.

Photos of his friends: out climbing, on the summit, at home.

Günther was a popular lad.

Photo of a mountain face: the Peitler, viewed from the north.

This first ascent, done in 1968, followed a direct line up the North Face to the summit. It was a great route and a tribute to Günther's vision.

A few scribbled lines – the draft of a poem.

I didn't know he wrote poems!

Letters.

From girl friends who had always wanted to go climbing with him.

I returned the journal to its place on the shelf. Next to it lay several medals from sports clubs.

Yes, he always had been a good runner.

Silver and gold medals.

He never thought much about victory celebrations.

The telegramme inviting him to Nanga Parbat.

Had Herrligkoffer really wanted competent climbing partnerships on his expedition?

Had he not proved on the mountain that the contrary was the case?

He had removed us from his summit assault plan.

A photo of the Rupal Face.

When you have stood together with a companion on the summit of a mountain it is painful to look at the photograph of the mountain on your own. When I think about Nanga Parbat now, Günther comes alive for me.

A few letters from Camp 3. We were snowed in. Avalanches, storms and cold. Descent impossible.

Günther had been one of the few who still believed in our summit vision.

Empty pages.

They had been earmarked for the account of the high point of his climbing career, for the Rupal Face of Nanga Parbat.

More photos: Günther at Camp 3.

We had never had so much free time than at that camp.
Günther at Base Camp, roasting a piece of ox meat on a spit.
He always was a good cook.
Günther on the summit of Heran Peak.
His first 6000m summit.
Günther beneath the Merkl Couloir.
He took the lead on the Rupal Face, right up to the top camp.
Günther on the exit pitches of the Rupal Face.
Right up to the end he shared the trail-breaking with me.
Günther with a heavy rucksack.
He carried more than 15kg up to Camp 4.
The Kleine Fermeda.
Our first summit together.
Nanga Parbat.
Our last.
There was also a charcoal sketch done by the artist Paluselli in autumn 1966. Günther had met him one day when soloing the North Ridge of the Cimone della Pala. The artist and the climber had become good friends.
Now Paluselli was dead, too. His mountain hut was abandoned and derelict. Perhaps there was no room for a madman in our 'Fit for Fun' society.
Another picture of Nanga Parbat.
It was the time that we had spent together on the mountain that made Nanga Parbat so important to me. This mountain was inextricably linked with my own destiny.
Another charcoal sketch. This time with a written dedication:
'Günther! What you achieved today can never be repeated. You are a hero – or a madman. Paluselli.'
Today, whenever I am out in the mountains, Günther is with me. We are still climbing partners.

Günther Messner. Sketch by Paluselli.

Years Later

In 1971 I visited the Nanga Parbat region again, high up in the Diamir Valley.

I was with Uschi von Kienlin, the wife of Max von Kienlin, who had looked after me tirelessly since my return from the 1970 expedition. We were visiting my rescuers.

In the summer of 1971 Uschi and I had fallen in love.

Peter Scholz, the warm-hearted Munich man, died a short while later on the Peuterey Ridge on Mont Blanc. Felix Kuen went to Mount Everest with Herrligkoffer in 1972. In 1974 he took his own life. No one knows why. Werner Heim also went on the 1972 Everest expedition. In 1986 he had a bad fall in the Karwendel, broke his back and was paralysed. Wolfi Bitterling also suffered serious disabilities after an

312

accident. After the arguments surrounding the 1970 Nanga Parbat Expedition, Karl Maria Herrligkoffer emerged victorious and went on to organize several further expeditions: to Mount Everest, Kanch, K2 and again to Nanga Parbat. He died in 1991 in Munich, at the age of 75 without ever having reached any of the highest summits of the Himalaya. In Germany, he came to symbolize Himalayan mountaineering. Michl Anderl, Gert Mändl and Hermann Kühn are also dead now. Some of the 1970 team I have lost contact with; others I meet on a regular basis, amongst them Jürgen Winkler, Gerd Baur, Elmar Raab and Peter Vogler. Hans Saler is still on his travels, usually somewhere in South America. He has found his peace and his answers in a lifetime of travelling the world.

In 1978 I climbed Nanga Parbat for the second time, solo and by a new route. It was and remains the boldest climb of my life.

In 1999 Hermann Buhl's ice axe was found at the summit of Nanga Parbat.

The excuses made by those who had doubted his claim came a little too late.

In 2000 I succeeding in climbing another new route on the North Face of Nanga Parbat, alpine-style, with a few friends from South Tyrol.

With the passing of the years I have become more cautious in my movements, more modest in my objectives and more selective in my choice of companions.

My brother Hubert, a doctor, with whom I made a traverse of the Greenland Ice Cap, was with me on my 2000 Nanga trip. Like Günther and I, as a lad Hubert had also slept in hayricks in the fields and later on rock ledges, in high camps and caves. *We both knew that it was only by accepting joint responsibility for our actions, by suffering the pain of hunger and cold together, that we could create a common bond. Those people, who, like Herrligkoffer, sought to gain forced entry into our dangerous paradise and to take what did not belong to them, were excluded. We viewed them with suspicion.*

Despite improved knowledge and better technology, no one has yet been able to repeat our route on the Rupal Face, although it has seen a dozen attempts.

Some of them also ended in tragedy.

In spite of everything, it is nonsense to speak of 'the curse of Nanga Parbat'. If it has become a mountain of destiny, then it has done so not because a demon rules the mountain but because the mountain is so infinitely bigger than we humans.

It was good to be able to show Hubert this world, this majestic mountain, on whose flanks I still felt lost and alone.

Bibliography

Bechtold, Fritz, *Deutsche am Nanga Parbat. Der Angriff 1934* (Verlag F. Bruckmann, Munich 1935)

Deutsche Himalaja-Stiftung Munich (eds) *Nanga Parbat. Berg der Kameraden.* Report of the 1938 German Himalaya Expedition (Union Deutsche Verlagsgesellschaft Berlin Roth & Co., Berlin 1943)

Dyhrenfurth, G.O., *Das Buch vom Nanga Parbat.* The story of the first ascent (Nymphenburger Verlagshaus, Munich 1954)

Herrligkoffer, Karl M., *Kampf und Sieg am Nanga Parbat. Die Bezwingung der höchsten Steilwand der Erde* (Spectrum Verlag, Stuttgart–Salzburg–Zürich 1971)

Herrligkoffer, Karl M., *Nanga Parbat. Sieben Jahrzehnte Gipfelkampf in Sonnenglut und Eis* (Ullstein Verlag, Frankfurt/Main–Berlin 1967)

Herrligkoffer, Karl M., *Nanga Parbat 1953* (J. F. Lehmanns Verlag, Munich 1954)

Herrligkoffer, Karl M., *Der letzte Schritt zum Gipfel. Kampf und Sieg im Himalaja* (Robert Bardtenschlager Verlag, Reutlingen 1958)

Herrligkoffer, Karl M. (ed.), *Im Banne des Nanga Parbat*, (J. F. Lehmanns Verlag, Munich 1953)

Merkl, Willy, *Ein Weg zum Nanga Parbat* (Bergverlag Rudolf Rother, Munich 1936)

Messner, Reinhold, *Die rote Rakete am Nanga Parbat.* Script for a film that can never be shown (Nymphenburger Verlagshandlung, Munich 1971)

Ruef, Karl, *Felix Kuen – auf den Gipfeln der Welt* (Leopold Stocker Verlag, Graz and Stuttgart 1972)

Schaefer, Hermann, *Die weiße Kathedrale. Abenteuer Nanga Parbat* (Nymphenburger Verlagshandlung, Munich 1987)

MORE MESSNER TITLES FROM THE MOUNTAINEERS BOOKS

Everest: Expedition to the Ultimate
Messner's account of his first ascent on Everest, made without supplemental oxygen. One of the best pieces of Everest literature, as voted by *Outside* magazine readers.

The Crystal Horizon: Everest— The First Solo Ascent
The extraordinary story of Messner's solo ascent of Everest without oxygen. One of *National Geographic* magazine's "100 Greatest Adventure Books of All Time."

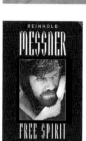

Reinhold Messner, Free Spirit: A Climber's Life
In a revealing autobiography, one of the most disciplined climbers of our time reflects on his remarkable career.

OTHER TITLES YOU MIGHT ENJOY FROM THE MOUNTAINEERS BOOKS

The Beckoning Silence, *Joe Simpson*
Questioning the pursuit to which he has devoted his entire life, Simpson attempts the north face of the Eiger—a final adventure that would itself be touched by tragedy.

The Flame of Adventure, *Simon Yates*
Is it only fun if you can die? World-class climber Simon Yates' stories take you inside the mind games that climbers play.

Nanga Parbat Pilgrimage: The Lonely Challenge, *Hermann Buhl*
Autobiography of Hermann Buhl, whose solo, unaided climb of Nanga Parbat is thought to be a greater achievement than Hillary and Norgay's summit of Everest.

Available at fine bookstores and outdoor stores, by phone at 800-553-4453, or on the Web at *www.mountaineersbooks.org*

THE MOUNTAINEERS BOOKS

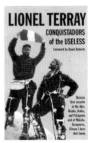